IT Automation

The Quest for Lights Out

▼ Data Warehousing: Architecture and Implementation
  Mark Humphries, Michael W. Hawkins, Michelle C. Dy

▼ Software Development: Building Reliable Systems
  Marc Hamilton

▼ IT Automation: The Quest for Lights Out
  Howie Lyke with Debra Cottone

▼ IT Organization: Building a Worldclass Infrastructure
  Harris Kern, Dr. Stuart D. Galup with Guy Nemiro

▼ High Availability: Design, Techniques and Processes
  Michael Hawkins, Floyd Piedad

HARRIS KERN'S ENTERPRISE COMPUTING INSTITUTE

IT Automation

The Quest for Lights Out

Howie Lyke
with Debra Cottone

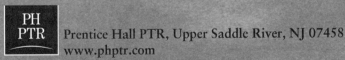

Prentice Hall PTR, Upper Saddle River, NJ 07458
www.phptr.com

Editorial/Production Supervision: *Mary Sudul*
Acquisitions Editor: *Greg Doench*
Editorial Assistant: *Mary Treacy*
Marketing Manager: *Bryan Gambrel*
Manufacturing Manager: *Alexis R. Heydt*
Cover Design Direction: *Jerry Votta*
Cover Design: *Talar Agasyan*
Composition: *FASTpages*
Series Design: *Gail Cocker-Bogusz*

Prentice Hall books are widely used by corporations and government agencies for training, marketing, and resale.

The publisher offers discounts on this book when ordered in bulk quantities.
For more information, contact Corporate Sales Department, Phone: 800-382-3419; fax: 201-236-714; email: corpsales@prenhall.com or write Corporate Sales Department, Prentice Hall PTR, One Lake Street, Upper Saddle River, NJ 07458.

Printed in the United States of America

10 9 8 7 6 5 4 3 2

ISBN 0-13-013786-3

Prentice-Hall International (UK) Limited, *London*
Prentice-Hall of Australia Pty. Limited, *Sydney*
Prentice-Hall Canada Inc., *Toronto*
Prentice-Hall Hispanoamericana, S.A., *Mexico*
Prentice-Hall of India Private Limited, *New Delhi*
Prentice-Hall of Japan, Inc., *Tokyo*
Simon & Schuster Asia Pte. Ltd., *Singapore*
Editora Prentice-Hall do Brasil, Ltda., *Rio de Janeiro*

Though this is my second involvement in a publication of this sort, it is my first as the sole author. Many close friends and family have given so that I may achieve this—for me—a monumental task.

But the largest giver of all is my son, Darien.
To him I dedicate this book.
I love you, DJ.

Contents

Chapter 4

Design and Planning   51

Tables

Figures

Index   153

Foreword

By Debra S. Cottone
Editor, *Lights Out*

There are many books, articles, and reference materials about data center technologies. So, when Howie Lyke approached me with the opportunity to edit a book on data center automation, I wondered who could possibly want or need another technical manual with limited shelf life.

I soon learned that Howie's book would be about *people and the processes they use to choose, infuse, and implement* technology successfully. These concepts would be illustrated by stories about good and bad choices from experiences with clients of all sizes. The book would offer practical, field-tested exercises and methods.

In addition, Howie wanted *Lights Out* to address the management of change due to increased automation. And, he wanted to emphasize the communications required to build support both for the proposed automation and the changes it would bring.

If Howie accomplished half of his vision, he would write a valuable book. Then again, the concepts he talked about are given lip service by many IT professionals. I took him seriously because I had seen his work:

> *I met Howie when we were on separate assignments for the same client. I was working on the selection process for a new billing and customer care system. Howie had been engaged*

to bring the company's data operations to a "world class" standard. From the very beginning, he focused on relationships first, processes second, and technology third, though many days it looked like all three at once.

Although Howie had the requisite technical knowledge, he knew that technology would not solve the problems. He understood that he would not deliver the expected results without the support, trust, and engagement of all the players: data center operations, applications development, vendors, the executive in charge, and more. Observant and alert, Howie was continually gathering information about the company's culture and decision-making processes, relationships and their history, successes and failures, and operating norms. In turn, he made it a high priority to communicate his purpose, work with and engage staff and users, and keep the executive in charge informed.

By definition, the project was going to generate change. For example, it required the development and documentation of process architectures to support new and existing technologies. The new processes would require that employees change what they did and how they did it. Howie's efforts to understand and engage key personnel before and during design and deployment paid off in their acceptance of the required changes.

Of course, the client's "world class" standard needed to be met while Howie ran the on-going data center operations, supported the good work previously accomplished by existing staff, and put out the daily fires of an operation sorely in need of enhancement. In the end, Howie's engagement was successful, although not without its challenges and setbacks; when a problem surfaced, he received immediate support. I observed that Howie not only said the right words about people and process, he did the right things to build relationships and manage change.

Howie Lyke is a "street smart" IT professional and his book, *Lights Out,* is a practical guide to data center automation. It isn't theory and it isn't technology-focused. It's about people, processes, and the knowledge born of experience in data centers all over the world. The lessons Howie learned and documented will have broad application potential for many years to come. That's why anyone who is thinking or learning about data center automation will both read and use *Lights Out* – not once, but over and over again.

Preface

▶ Introduction

As new and enhanced information technologies penetrate the enterprise at increasing rates, the IT executives who recommend and approve them are doing so with higher and higher expectations for increased automation and measurable returns.

In an automated enterprise, managers expect lower personnel requirements, greater reliability, quicker problem resolution, less downtime, and lower maintenance costs. With these benefits, no wonder the investment in new technologies continues to escalate. However, the complexities of distributed computing, integrated systems including outsourced service bureaus, and heterogeneous data centers have made these benefits difficult to come by. In many cases, the new data center environment is more manually intensive and more expensive to operate than ever before.

Lights Out, in its purest definition, is not a perfectly attainable goal. This book presents a methodology for achieving the highest level of automation possible.

This book addresses the problem with practical advice, guidelines and tools that will lead you through the analysis, planning, and implementation of data center automation projects. The process begins with an exercise that develops realistic expectations for a level of automation that you can expect to achieve in your data center environments.

Next, the book guides you through a gap analysis and the identification of automation requirements. *Lights Out* addresses IT organization and project staffing issues, followed by a thorough review of the steps, options, and considerations of the design phase. The particular challenges of planning an automation project are defined in the section on project planning.

Most IT managers will need to "sell" their automation initiative to upper management. This book details the steps and techniques required, including the development of financial plans and strategies. Of equal importance, you will find valuable, easy-to-apply tips and communications approaches to package and sell the total project.

This book also contains experience-proven guidelines for successful deployment and post-implementation improvement.

▶ Data Center Definition

A data center is more than a computer room full of hardware and software. In the new enterprise, "the network is the data center." The data center is comprised of the network and virtually everything attached to it—the computer center, workstations, desktops, and all related components:

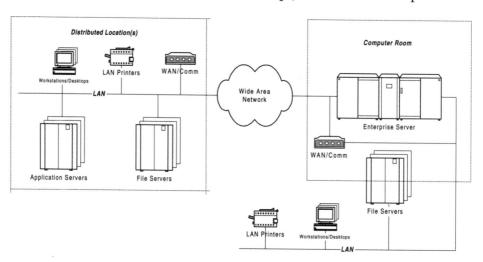

Figure I–1   Data Center Diagram

Figure I-1 depicts a data center spanning two locations: a central area where the main computer room is located and a remote facility that is connected to the components in the computer room via a Wide Area Network (WAN). The central computer room contains enterprise (database), application, and file servers, communications equipment, and supporting hardware.

The distributed servers in the location where the computer room resides are located within and outside the computer room. In general, distributed servers may be located anywhere from a central computer room to the most remote locales of the enterprise, and at any point in between.

Data center production processes manage most if not all of the components shown in the Data Center Diagram. Take, for example, the distribution of software from the server to the desktop. Software distribution models, which consist of a combination of software and technical processes, centrally house and manage applications and make the software automatically available to other systems and to desktop users. The technical and administrative processes to effectively manage software distribution are executed by the data center.

As you read this book, remember that the term "data center" refers to the network, all of its components as illustrated above, and all of the technical and administrative processes that it executes.

▶ Target Audience—Who Should Read This Book

The IT Executive

IT managers and executives, from director to CIO, will benefit from the content and layout of this book. Executive-level managers are responsible for providing direction, reviewing progress, and making key decisions regarding initiatives targeted at automating operations. To fulfill these management responsibilities, many rely solely upon their intuitive management skills and past experience. *Lights Out* serves as a reference guide and a useful resource to validate intuition and augment experience gained in different data center environments. In its pages, IT executives will find a thorough guide to decision-making, including key questions to ask in each phase of the project, from planning and budgeting through execution and fine-tuning. As a deskside reference manual, *Lights Out* can be utilized to challenge assumptions, improve planning, and validate checkpoints and milestones being established as realistic and achievable.

The Operations Manager

Operations managers, tasked with managing front-line personnel and executing projects, will also use this book as a reference guide. However, the operations manager will reference this material from a different perspective. Whereas the IT executive provides direction, review, and approval, the operations manager develops the project, sets expectations and manages implementation to meet the executive's focus on the IT mission, budget, and corporate objectives. To succeed, the manager must dive into the dirty details and follow each one of the disciplines described in this book. The manager should focus particularly on technical evaluation, planning, and associated cost management. The manager must then "sell" his/her proposal to the executive(s), without raising expectations beyond realistic delivery. And if that's not enough, should he/she be successful in the sale—be careful what you ask for—the manager is then responsible to execute the plan and stick around to make it work!

Like the executive, the manager relies upon his/her intuitive management skills and past experience. All too often, one or more areas of discipline described in this book do not receive the appropriate level of attention, and the project is delayed, is underfunded, or proceeds without sufficient senior management support. *Lights Out* will take the guesswork out of planning, selling, and executing a successful data center automation initiative.

Infrastructure Personnel

Wherever they are located and whatever their position, all data center staff will benefit from reading *Lights Out*, by understanding how they can add value to an automation initiative and how they might be asked to participate. Any data center employee anticipating a pending automation project should use this book to prepare for the project. In addition, employees who think that their company should be investing in additional automation can use this book to initiate a project. In *Lights Out*, they will find the tips, tools, and a process to focus their manager on the right issues in the right way.

Consultants and Technology Vendors

Individuals who make a living in data center and infrastructure consulting or product and service sales will benefit from the practical advice, tips, and field-tested methodology described in *Lights Out*. They can use this material to validate previously used approaches and refresh their proposals. Since *Lights Out* is written from the perspective of the internal IT manager, the consultants and sales personnel will pick up valuable contextual sensitivity that should help them tailor communications to reflect real business issues. *Lights Out* deals with concerns that every thoughtful CIO and Infrastructure Services Manager will face as they consider additional automation and the investment in new technologies. In fact, *Lights Out* will help the consultant and salesperson to identify key questions that will or should be asked. As a result, proposals and on-going client interactions will be more relevant, effective, and productive.

The IT Management Students and Instructors

Students of information services and technologies will benefit from the practical, real-world reference materials, information, and examples contained in *Lights Out*. All students, full-time or part-time, about to begin an IT career or mid-career and climbing the management ladder, will gain access to the lessons learned automating data center operations in a myriad of organizations. By completing the exercises, students will develop valuable skills and understand the steps required to successfully scope, plan, and sell an automation initiative. By reading each chapter, students will expand their IT knowledge base. By discussing the materials in the classroom, students will validate their understanding versus the experiences and knowledge of their colleagues.

Instructors of IT can use *Lights Out* to teach the skills and processes that will be required in the real world of enterprise automation. The material lends itself particularly well to role playing, classroom discussion, and group assignments. Case studies may be developed, wherein the instructor supplies the case facts and the students use the materials to evaluate automation opportunities, scope and plan the project, develop the cost analysis, and role play the sales pitch.

▶ Reader Assumptions

This book assumes that you understand general IT industry terms, have knowledge of or experience managing or working in a data center and supporting infrastructure, and understand the difference among mainframe, client/server, and distributed platform computing. In addition, I assume that you have basic project planning and project management experience and skills.

▶ How to Read This Book

This book presents a methodology to plan and execute data center, infrastructure automation projects. This methodology is best represented by Figure I-2:

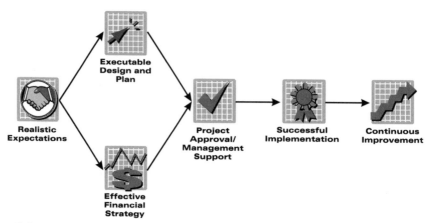

Figure I–2   Lights Out Execution Methodology

In summary, the methodology takes you through the various phases of the project, and the chapters of the book are mapped to follow the methodology. In Chapters One and Two, the reader will define the purpose and scope of the automation project with a series of exercises that set realistic expectations, identify the problems and opportunities, and establish automation requirements. In Chapter Three, IT organization and project staffing issues and key considerations are highlighted. The details of design and a high-level project planning approach are presented in Chapter Four. The methodology suggests that the development of an effective financial strategy, described in Chapter Five, can be undertaken on a parallel track with design and project planning.

The next step involves packaging and selling the project to management. Chapter Six reviews the importance of communications throughout the project and offers a template for the final presentation prior to approval. Deployment, or a successful implementation, is described in Chapter Seven. Chapter Seven covers the post-implementation phase, which is referred to as continuous improvement.

To repeat, each chapter in this book maps to the methodology and to the symbols associated with each phase, as Table I-1 shows:

Table I–1   Methodology and Chapter Mapping

Methodology Step-by-Step	Chapter Reference
Realistic Expectations	Chapter One: Lights Out Exposed Chapter Two: Gap Analysis Chapter Three: The Organization
Executable Design and Plan	Chapter Four: Design and Planning
Effective Financial Strategy	Chapter Five: Financial Planning
Project Approval/Management Support	Chapter Six: Communicating and Presenting the Plan
Successful Implementation	Chapter Seven: Deployment and Continuous Improvement
Continuous Improvement	Chapter Seven: Deployment and Continuous Improvement

Each chapter begins with an introductory section containing the purpose of the chapter, orientation to the methodology, a narrative of a real situation that illustrates the application of the steps described in the chapter, and key questions that are addressed in the narrative.

The material is presented in several formats to allow for different learning styles. Each chapter contains some combination of narratives, tables, and figures that depict the processes.

Acknowledgments

The author/writer assignment of this book insufficiently characterizes Debra Cottone's role in the production of this book. More than just a writer, Debra gave me a way to present my "real world" experiences and make my hard-won learnings comprehensible to my readers. She did it by sifting through my stories, experiences and project descriptions. She questioned my assumptions and pressed me for clarity. Then, she synthesized it all into an overall methodology that readers can use to organize, structure, and manage automation projects. The methodology had dual purposes; we used it as a road map to define and write the chapters of this book.

In addition, Debra provided much valuable content, writing significant portions of every chapter including the preface and introduction. I used many of her suggestions to spiff up old tools and create new ones. Finally, Debra believed in the power of story telling. She encouraged me to write the stories at the beginning of each chapter and to pepper the narrative with real experiences.

To Debra, my great friend and collaborator, thanks for all of your contributions, but most of all thanks for the learning.

Thanks to Ken Lee for having the lunacy to let me lead it all the way.

Special thanks to my parents, Loren and Frances Lyke, for their undying lifetime-ful of support and love.

Debt and servitude to our friend and supporter, Bill Brooks, who scrambled around at the last minute to help deliver this book.

Special thanks to Tom Schumacher, whose contributions helped get this book completed and whose energy and dedication helps keep my business alive and thriving.

Special recognition to Michael Hawkins, part of the backbone of this series.

"Lights Out"—Exposed

Planning and executing a successful automation project begins by developing realistic expectations for the purpose and scope of the initiative:

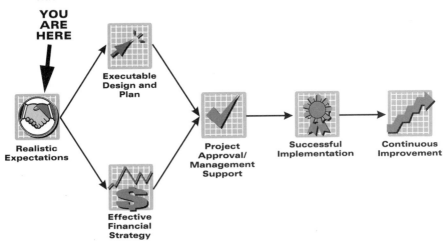

A *few years ago, I spent several months re-architecting the data center operations of a nine-plus billion dollar cash receipt company in Hong Kong. I was contracted to study their mission-critical computing environment, to develop a new architecture, and to prepare the transition plan from a legacy to client/server platform that needed to operate at a*

"lights out" automation standard. My assignment was driven by a comprehensive initiative (already underway) to rewrite their mission-critical applications on a client/server platform.

The "lights out" objectives were explicit: reduce head count and ultimately the overall cost of the data center. The challenge was a little scary for me. Although the customer's objectives were succinct, obviously, no one involved had a clear or common understanding of what "lights out" actually meant. To fulfill my contract successfully and satisfy my customer, I had to develop, articulate, and establish the appropriate level of expectation surrounding their "lights out" automation fantasy. To do so, I used the exercises that are described in this chapter.

I completed my mission in Hong Kong and delivered a new architecture for their data center infrastructure and a related plan to make the transition. This data center operation was sizeable. Implementation required the transition of 96 minimainframes to new client/server applications and platform over a two- to three-year period. About two years later, on a visit to Hong Kong, the CIO pointed to the architecture and plan manuals that were still sitting on the top of his desk and proudly reported that over 75% of the plan, technical and process, had been implemented. Given the magnitude of the initiative, their progress was a resounding success. I strongly believe that this positive message and outcome was (in addition to good planning and project management) a direct result of the expectations set early in the project using the exercises described in this chapter.

 As you read this chapter and apply the ideas and exercises to your environment and challenges, expect to fully qualify and answer the following key questions:

- "What areas of my operation can I realistically expect to automate given my budget, company culture, and related resources?"

- "Once I've identified the areas in my operation I can expect to automate, what level of automation can I realistically expect to achieve?"

The term "lights out" has been used in the IT industry for many years in different contexts. Lights out operation in a data center environment may be defined as:

> *The automation of manual activities to limit requirements for human intervention and consistently deliver desired results.*

The automation of data center operations to a lights out standard requires the identification of specific requirements and decisions concerning the desirable level of automation. What processes are good candidates for automation? What realistic results may be obtained? How will the changes affect operations, budgets, and staffing? Can the cost of automation be justified?

This chapter contains key considerations for data center managers and architects who are analyzing opportunities for automation. These considerations include (a) the infrastructure components that are candidates for automation, (b) the level of complexity involved in automation, and (c) the realistic objectives for automation of each component. An assessment of these considerations will lead to a high-level list of components that may be suitable for automation in a particular data center environment.

Identifying the Components and Complexity of Lights Out Operations

 All the infrastructure components in your data center may be suitable for automation. Table 1-1 contains a list of components, brief definitions of each, and the factors that affect the complexities involved in automating them. In this context, the term "complexity" is a measure of the staffing requirements and coordination, the number of technical requirements, the time needed to evaluate alternative solutions, the technical implementation, maintenance of the implementation, and associated costs. Engage your staff in the evaluation and decision concerning the complexity level of each component. Use Table 1-1 to lead a discussion that results in a complexity level assignment for each of the components in your data center.

Table 1–1 Data Center Components for Automation Consideration

Component	Definition	Auto-Complexity Level (Low/Medium/High)
Technical Architecture		
Performance Monitoring and Capacity Planning	Global view of network and system resource utilization, which identifies potential performance problems and provides sufficient computing resources to support current and future business requirements	Medium to High—*Many tools are available to address the automation requirements. The complexity level increases with multiple platform considerations.*
Disk Capacity Management	Process to effectively manage disk usage	Low to Medium—*Many tools are available. Easy to manage through homegrown scripts and processes. Complexity increases as the automation requirements are integrated into an enterprise management initiative.*
Storage Management	Backup/restore, catalogue, and storage process to effectively manage disk and tape archival requirements	Medium to High—*Many tools exist today to address the automation requirements. The complexity level increases with multiple platform considerations.*
Event Monitoring	Process to monitor an event on a system, a network, a database, an application (e.g., a fault, a threshold), which then alerts a centralized management function	Medium to High—*This process is often confused with performance and capacity requirements. Tools will accommodate well defined requirements. Again, the complexity level increases with multiple platform considerations.*
Network Management	Process to monitor the network, to perform trouble-shooting and to manage network configuration and growth	Medium to High—*Many tools exist today to address the automation requirements. Complexity is added when fragmented network groups (i.e., separate domains) manage the enterprise.*

Table 1–1   Data Center Components for Automation Consideration
(continued)

Component	Definition	Auto-Complexity Level (Low/Medium/High)
Access (Security) Management	Process to address user security for application, database, and transaction-level access	High—*Requires centralization of all access administration processes for mission-critical applications. Enterprise tools are custom installations*
Job Scheduling	Process to schedule jobs, perform job-restart, and check job dependency in a distributed environment	Low to Medium—*Batch scheduling tools, even in the UNIX environment, are well established and mature. The complexity level increases with multiple platform considerations.*
Version Release	Process to change and maintain the release of objects, e.g., System Software and Application Software, between the test and the production environments	Medium to High—*Many tools exist today to address these requirements. The complexity level increases with multiple platform considerations.*
Software Distribution	Process to update and maintain distributed software	Low to High—*Platform specific tools are available to address these requirements. To establish one automated process/system to manage software distribution over multiple platforms is nearly impossible. Automation requires a separate process for each platform.*
Process Architecture		
Production Acceptance	Process that identifies the operational requirements to implement and manage new and changing applications	Low to Medium—*This is an administrative process. However, document management systems can be created within the existent environment to standardize and automate inputs, outputs, and information. Forms and routing can be addressed by Intranet type installations.*

Table 1–1 Data Center Components for Automation Consideration
(continued)

Component	Definition	Auto-Complexity Level (Low/Medium/High)
Problem Management	A centralized process to manage and resolve user network, application, and system problems	Medium to High—*Standard help desk tools can address rudimentary requirements with minimal customization. Complexity and cost increase when requirements necessitate the custom installation of commercial products. Complexity escalates further when other automated monitoring tools are integrated into the problem management system.*
Change Management	A process that coordinates all changes that affect the production environment	Low to Medium—*This is an administrative process; however, document management systems can be created within the existent environment to standardize and automate inputs, outputs, and information. Forms and routing can be addressed by Intranet type installations.*
Asset Management	Process to query, discover, track, and store enterprise computing resources, including hardware, operating systems, and applications	High—*Asset management is composed of numerous elements. Some elements are suitable for the development of data management systems in the existent environment to standardize and automate inputs, outputs, and information.*
Disaster Recovery	Process to enable recovery in the event a disaster should render mission-critical systems inoperable	High—*The disaster recovery process is supported by high-availability technology. The disaster recovery plan includes the identification and standardization of procedures and decision-making criteria; certain elements of the plan may be automated.*

Automation—The Reality Check

The high-level analysis of components that are suitable for automation requires consideration of both complexity and obtainable results. Table 1-2 repeats the list of data center components, followed by unrealistic expectations (Column Two) and real, obtainable results (Column Three). The "obtainable results" column is designed to provide a baseline expectation that may be adjusted according to the resources available for investment in each automation project. Again, involve your staff in developing a high-level list of expectations for the automation of each of these components. You may eliminate some of the components from consideration as a result.

Table 1–2 Automation Components—Reality Check

Component	Unrealistic Model	Obtainable Results
Technical Architecture		
Performance Monitoring and Capacity Planning	Automatically capture resource utilization (system, disk, network bandwidth, cpu, i/o, database transaction) real-time Automatically locate the bottleneck or problems Automatically resolve or tune with no human intervention	Automatically capture resource utilization Automatically escalate and notify support personnel when threshold exceeds pre-defined limits and provide information or hints for further analysis Manual process and procedures to address troubleshooting
Disk Management	Automatically capture disk space thresholds Automatically add hard disk space to the system Automatically detect hard disk failures Automatically replace failures	Automatically capture disk space thresholds Automatically add hard disk space to the system Automatically detect hard disk failures Manually replace failures

Table 1–2 Automation Components—Reality Check *(continued)*

Component	Unrealistic Model	Obtainable Results
Storage Management	Backups automatically start at scheduled time on system labeled tapes.	Backups automatically start at scheduled time on system labeled tapes.
	Automatically restores data files for users.	Automatically restores data files for users.
	Robotic tape loading and archiving with built-in cataloging. Automatically organizes tapes for third-party vendor pick-up and delivery.	Robotic tape loading and archiving with built-in cataloging. Manual organization of tapes for third-party vendor pick-up and delivery.
	Automatically stores archives off-site.	Manual process to store archives off-site.
	Automatically contacts third-party vendor for return of tapes.	Manual contact third-party vendor for return of tapes.
Event Monitoring	Automated system to monitor the environment (network, database, application, etc.).	Automated system to monitor the environment.
	System automatically reacts and resolves problem using an information database.	System automatically reacts to problem by notifying support personnel without human intervention.
		Human intervention and/or expertise to resolve problem.
Network Management	Automatically configures hardware on the network.	Automatically provides monitoring data to feed the event monitoring process and output.
	Automatically determines upgrade requirements, e.g., model, size, etc.	Provides utilities for troubleshooting, capacity planning, and network configuration management.
	Automatically installs, configures, or tunes for optimal performance.	

Table 1–2   Automation Components—Reality Check *(continued)*

Component	Unrealistic Model	Obtainable Results
Access (Security) Management	An integrated online application to: Automatically handle requests, approvals, technical administration and auditing for user access processing to the network, system, database, application, and transaction levels.	Application that standardizes and automates inputs, outputs, and information to process requests and approval routing, providing auditability, for user access to the system, database, and transaction levels. Technical administration is centralized but still manual.
	Automatically detect, configure, and authorize access privileges for new applications introduced to the network, system, and database.	Manually detect, configure and authorize access privileges for new applications introduced to the network, system, and database.
	Automatic detection and reporting for security breach of network, system, database, and transaction levels.	Automatic detection and reporting for security breach of network, system, database, and transaction levels.
Job Scheduling	Automatically detect new application batch processes and schedules.	Manually detect new application batch processes and schedules.
	Automatically schedule jobs to run at the most optimal time.	Implement a manually configured schedule of jobs.
	Automatically check for dependencies.	Automatically check for dependencies.
	Automatically restart if failed processes.	Automatically restart if failed processes.
Version Release	Automatically detect configuration of new applications.	Manually detect configuration of new applications.
	Automatically track the configuration and "package" of objects to be changed.	Automatically track the configuration and "package" of objects to be changed.
	Automatically log and report changes.	Automatically log and report changes.
	Automatically grant appropriate authority to new applications.	Automatically grant appropriate authority to new applications.
	Automatically back out from a change if deemed unsuccessful.	Automatically back out from a release or change.

Table 1–2 Automation Components—Reality Check *(continued)*

Component	Unrealistic Model	Obtainable Results
Software Distribution	Automatically distribute software products from the server to the desktop. Automatically detect, track, and resolve license requirements, software releases, and client architecture.	Centralized administration for bug fixes, patches, upgrades. Reduced manual requirements for systems administration.
Process Architecture		
Production Acceptance	Automatically gather and meet operational requirements for new applications.	Implement document management system to standardize and automate inputs, outputs, and information.
Problem Management	Automatically detect problems anywhere in the enterprise. Automatically react to and resolve problems with no human intervention.	Implement system to log, track, escalate with, and report problems and their resolution. Manually react to and resolve problems.
Change Management	Automatically receive requests for change and determine potential impacts. Automatically gain approval and technical support. Automatically publishes change control notification. Automatically verifies status of changes and publishes.	Implement document management system to standardize and automate inputs, outputs, and information.
Asset Management	Automatically enter, track, and audit assets and end- of-life processes.	Implement system to standardize inputs, outputs, and information.
Disaster Recovery	When disaster strikes, all applications automatically shift to recovery site and continue to process with no interruption.	Good contingency plan providing recovery of mission-critical applications within the time frame specified in the plan.

Now that you have completed these exercises, you have a list of the components that are good candidates for automation in your data center. You have a sense of the complexity of the work required to automate those components. And you have realistic expectations about the level of automation you can achieve.

These realistic expectations have been developed for each component, but you still need to answer the question: What is the primary benefit we hope to gain from an automation initiative? How will I know that the project has been successful? The answer to these questions should be framed in a purpose statement for the initiative. This statement will become your key message as you refine the scope and requirements and inform management that you are researching an automation project. That you position the purpose of the project carefully is critical, since you will live with the expectations you set. Development of the purpose statement is another opportunity to engage your staff. Here is a sample purpose statement:

The purpose of the project is to automate the technical and process architectures so as to deliver more efficient processing, a reduction in the growth of staffing resources, and more effective operations management.

▶ The Two-Second Validation

However, before you go through the rigor of design and project planning for each of these components, you have one more filter to apply. This filter is simply a—thirty-thousand-foot—intuitive assessment of the feasibility of the automation projects. It's what I call "the two-second validation."

Although the assessment is largely intuitive, I have identified some questions to consider. The reason this is an intuitive process is that the data is largely situational and therefore varies from company to company and time to time. To validate the feasibility of any given initiative, ask yourself the following questions:

- Is there an executive-level directive to cut costs and headcount?
- Does the culture support technology investment to reduce operating expenses?
- Do you have funding in your budget for system management tools or any other type of automation?

- Could other budgeted items be postponed to free up funds for the automation project(s)?
- Do you have any positive momentum to build from?

If you think through your particular situation and review your list of components and likely candidates for automation, you will be able to apply the intuitive, two-second validation. This is a good time to sit down with your IT executive and get his or her input. Review your components list and expectations and the draft purpose statement. The purpose statement helps you define the opportunity. By engaging your executive now, you will set expectations early and get a flavor for the objections that she/he may raise later. Now you have support and input from your staff and boss, a qualified list of components, and a draft purpose statement to carry forward into the technical and financial planning steps described in upcoming chapters.

Gap Analysis

You have taken a high-level inventory of your data center's technical and administrative process components and developed expectations for automating them. In addition, you developed a draft purpose statement for the automation initiative that you are researching and you shared it with your IT executive. Now you need to refine your expectations and scope of work further by developing problem/opportunity statements associated with each component and developing your automation requirements. You are still in the first step of our methodology:

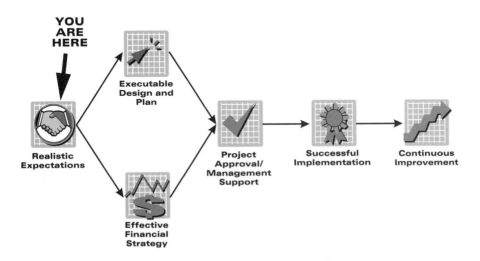

YOU ARE HERE

Realistic Expectations

Executable Design and Plan

Effective Financial Strategy

Project Approval/ Management Support

Successful Implementation

Continuous Improvement

One of my clients had a data center that evolved in two years from a couple of database servers to a roomful of business-critical database and application servers with hundreds of gigabytes of storage. The servers were connected to the business areas via a "spaghetti mess" of wire that included wires to wiring closets on other floors, multiple T1s to other locations, and telco service to USWest. It was a mess!

As with many growing IT organizations, the data center was simply regarded as a "computer room," a place to rack computers and network equipment. Security consisted of a cyberlock on the door. Production control consisted of the System Administrator and a controlled environment for power and temperature. The expenditures required to bring the data center up to par were repeatedly postponed. All available investment funds were allocated to development without parallel infrastructure investments, even though the servers were critical to 24x7 business operations.

As the operation grew, so did the problems. Servers were constantly unavailable as the operating systems and databases experienced problems, causing unscheduled reboots and maintenance. One day, one of the major database servers went down. It went down because someone entered the computer room, took a key to a production server cabinet, inserted it, and powered it down. What did the customer do? Whatever any self-respecting manager would do in a similar situation: blamed the hardware vendor. That's when I met the customer. Upon investigation, we found software developers littered throughout production space with no controls and an under-resourced operational staff with no production processes. The first order of business? Needs qualification and gap analysis.

 As you read this chapter and apply the ideas and exercises to your environment and challenges, expect to answer the following key questions:

- What is the current baseline of the data center?

- What are the problems and opportunities associated with the technical and administrative process components that I want to automate more fully?

- How does the baseline compare to the desired level of automation? Do you have good reasons to support the automation initiatives or are these proposals "nice-to-have's"?
- Who are the data center's end users? What are their business needs?
- How do business needs affect automation requirements?

Now that you have developed a working list of the components of your data center that seem suitable for a new level of automation, the next step is to examine and analyze the current level of automation versus the automation opportunity. Understanding and documenting the gap between the current situation and what is required (the desired state) is the basis for the technical planning described in Chapter 4. This documentation will also provide valuable assistance in financial planning and in selling the initiative to management.

▶ The Gap Model

The gap analysis consists of the following simple steps:

1. Document the Before picture—a description of current data center automation and the problems or opportunities associated with it.
2. Document the After picture—a description of the desired level of automation.
3. Document the Gap between Before and After.

The inputs and outputs of the gap analysis are summarized in Table 2-1. Tips for completing your gap analysis are contained in the sections that follow.

Table 2–1   Gap Analysis Steps

Step	Inputs	Activities or Process	Outputs
The "Before" Picture	List of current technical and administrative process components Automation expectations developed in Chapter 1 exercises	Inventory: Describe the current level of automation for each technical and administrative process component Diagnosis: Identify and list unresolved problems and opportunities for improvement	Matrix of current technical and administrative process components annotated with the current level of automation Problem and opportunity statements for each technical and administrative process component in the matrix
The "After" Picture	List of technical and administrative processes components with problem and opportunity statements Automation expectations developed in Chapter 1	Needs Analysis: Meet with user community to develop user requirements Meet with the applications development group to develop their requirements Meet with data center staff to validate system management software and operational requirements Automation Requirements: Meet with data center staff to develop automation requirements that address problems/opportunities Validation: Validate that the automation requirements support the needs of the user community, applications development group, system management, and operations Eliminate components or processes that are not associated with a problem or opportunity	Matrix of technical and administrative process components annotated with the proposed level of automation expressed as automation requirements, or identified as not suitable for automation Problem or opportunity statements that support the automation requirements
The "Gap"	Outputs from "Before" Picture (step 1) Outputs from "After" Picture (step 2)	Document the gaps between what is currently in place and what is proposed to meet your new automation requirements	Matrix outlining and highlighting the scope of your automation initiative

The "After" picture of the data center contains a detailed description of the level of automation for each technical and administrative process, and an associated problem or opportunity statement. The post-automation picture contrasted with the current situation highlights the gap. The plan is then established and contains the steps required to migrate from "Before" to "After." The plan and the problem and opportunity statements are used for obtaining funding and approval for the project and in project implementation. Once the post-automation or "After" picture is achieved, implementation is complete and continuous improvement begins.

Your Data Center Today—The Before Picture

The "before" picture of your data center is a description of the current level of automation for each technical and administrative process component, and a problem or opportunity statement that describes what can be fixed or improved via automation. Taking inventory and canvassing your staff for information develops the documentation. You can obtain the information in a meeting or by asking staff to submit written documentation. A meeting works well, since you also need to document the automation problems and/or opportunities associated with each component and process, and your staff should be a valuable resource in developing these ideas. I suggest that you describe the current level of automation for all components and processes, even those that you eliminated in the Chapter 1 exercises. After all, your staff may identify a problem or opportunity that you missed. Developing a complete "before" picture is an important first step in defining an automation initiative that is complete and justifiable.

The After Picture—The Lights Out Data Center

The "After" picture of your data center is a description of the proposed level of automation for each technical and administrative process component, and associated problem/opportunity statement(s). Development of the "After" picture starts by identifying the needs of three groups: end users, the applications development group in the IT department, and your own data center staff. The automation requirements are developed with your data center staff based upon problems or opportunities that you identified in the "Before" picture. The "After" picture is complete only after you have validated that the automation requirements support (or at a minimum do not adversely affect) the end-user, applications development, and data center needs. Additional automation that is not supported by a problem or opportunity statement is eliminated from consideration.

The next few sections provide details on developing and validating the "After" picture.

▶ Needs Analysis

Your data center probably evolved in response to needs expressed by users of the data center, as well as your company's expansion, business development needs, or organizational changes. Chances are that the original needs were informal (not documented) and that changes occurred in an evolutionary manner.

Here's a typical scenario. You have an existing mainframe or related legacy operation. A decision is made to install a client/server application. The application will serve large group(s) of users. It requires a place to be installed and something to sit on. The implementation will require hardware, facilities, staff to operate it, and some level of processes. Typically, the new application would be installed in the "computer room" containing the established legacy system. However, the client/server installation is segregated and developed independently, without taking advantage of the established processes and disciplines of the legacy operation. Thereafter, changes are made in reaction to requests from various user groups for better or additional operations services. No formal needs analysis occurs, and the development is ad hoc.

Additionally, technology is often inserted that is not based upon satisfying business requirements. IT professionals are typically techies. And techies love tech. IT staff may get whipped up over a new release of software or hardware that offers "bigger and better features" that drive "wouldn't it be great if we could take this widgit and shove it in this hole" purchasing decisions. This approach is "leading with technology." Leading with technology results in myopic technical decisions that don't consider standards, skill set investment, long-term support, and the ability to measure success, performance, and/or cost versus benefit.

To ensure a successful automation initiative, give the needs analysis time and attention. And be certain that the needs you identify are translated into requirements that will help your company achieve its business objectives. You will work with users to create and clarify their needs, and you will work with management to validate them. Management will help you separate desires or "nice to have's" from legitimate needs and match needs with the company's business plans. Management may also validate the accuracy of the issues raised. Finally, you will incorporate the needs of IT—both applications development and data center infrastructure operations.

Obtaining Business User Requirements

Here is a simple sequence of actions that will help you identify and focus on the real business needs and requirements that are important to your data center:

1. Understand your enterprise.
2. Identify the business units.
3. Identify a key contact person in each of the business units.
4. Interview each key person.
5. Summarize key responses.
6. Translate specific expectations as "requirements."
7. Validate the new "requirements" with the key contact in the business units and with management.

Understanding your enterprise is simply taking stock of what kind of company your data center supports. The key questions are: what kind of company is this, anyway? What are the mission statement, long-term goals, and annual objectives? Who are the company's key customers? Key products? Is the company manufacturing, engineering, marketing, or technology-based?

Understanding the enterprise may seem rudimentary, but I am constantly surprised at the lack of overall perspective many IT personnel, particularly those in the data center, have about the kind of company they serve. When you join a data center operation or have been managing it for awhile, you can easily get quickly mired in the details of its operation and become distanced from the real business of the company. A recent experience highlights the point:

Not long ago, I huddled with my technical staff and vendors trying to solve a general performance problem on a data warehouse. The type of data and what it was being used for was not our focus. Nope. All we knew or cared about was the fact that queries were running slowly. The inputs we dealt with were charts and trends of CPU percentage versus query counts versus disk i/o, the time of day, where the moon and stars were lined up, you name it. Unfortunately, we didn't have context. We didn't consider the importance, timeliness, and uses of the information in the context of what the company does to run its core business. The fact that we were operating a decision support system designed to drive key business information to marketing managers was irrelevant. Or was it?

Oh, by the way, this is a marketing company. Marketing is what this company does. Marketing is how this company creates and grows revenue. It doesn't manufacture hardware, engineer networks, or develop new products. We couldn't define successful performance without the business context. How slow was too slow? What performance would be fast enough?

Understanding what kind of company you work for will help you derive more accurate requirements from users and will provide additional benefits as well:

- It will help you orient yourself and get your mind-set for the conversations you will have with the user community.
- It will help provide the link you will need between the technical issues and how they will benefit the business when selling your initiative.
- It will help you organize requirements obtained from the business users.

Steps two to four involve identifying the key internal customers in the business units and interviewing them to understand their current and future business requirements. Business units are the major functions of the company such as Sales and Marketing, Finance, Customer Service, Engineering, Operations, etc. Employees in these units or departments are end users, or business users. Business users impose requirements by demanding and using the applications (and data) hosted by the servers located in the data center. Their needs drive data center requirements for functionality, availability, response time, and connectivity, and may affect the automation requirements.

 An organization chart is a good place to start to identify the business units and their key representatives. Even if you know the main players in your company, a good idea is to re-orient yourself with a fresh look at the formal organization. Use the organization chart to develop a list of interviewees. Validate the list with others in IT and management. Contact them and inform them that you are in the midst of planning an upgrade to the data center and are taking stock of user needs and expectations. Tell them that their perspective of your operation and specific new requirements is important to you.

Prepare for the interviews. Develop a form (ideas are in Table 2–2) so that you capture and document the information accurately and are able to make good use of their time.

Table 2–2 Sample User Questionnaire

Sample Questions	Typical Answers	Expect to Learn	Needs/ Requirements
For what kinds of services do you rely on the data center?	Reporting Change Mgmt Technical Implementation	Highlights perspectives the user community has of the data center and its role	Missing processes
Whom do you interface with most from the data center?	Production Control	Provides an outline of your data center's key interfaces to the user community	None
What do you like best from the service you receive from the data center?	Friendly staff	Highlights the level of customer service expected/desired	None
In what areas do you have the most problems with the data center?	System Performance Slow troubleshooting Unavailable off-hour personnel Missed problems with production schedule System Availability	Highlights level of production quality expected	Performance increases Off-hour support Automation needs High Availability

Table 2–2   Sample User Questionnaire *(continued)*

Sample Questions	Typical Answers	Expect to Learn	Needs/ Requirements
When do you need access to the application?	Our service center is open from 7:00 a.m. to 10:00 p.m. daily, 365 days per year	Identifies time and hours of use Validates current specification	System availability
Do you anticipate changing your hours of operation?	Actually, we are migrating to 24 by 7 next year	Identifies emerging need	Future system availability
How many users do you have and where are they located? What are your plans, if any, for expansion?	We currently have 500 users in Denver, 200 in Salt Lake City, and another 100 in San Francisco. We plan to expand the Salt Lake facility by 400 seats next year.	Establishes the baseline for scalability	Scalability
What applications do your employees use?	Netscape 4.0, Microsoft Outlook, the order entry system, and the corporate fax system	Validates desktop images	Will uncover needs for new technical or process components

Note that the interviews can be formal or informal. In certain situations, the type of information shown in Table 2–2 above can be derived from a chat over lunch. In others, formal structured time must be given to the process and the output. Whatever forum you use, validate the results of the interview with the person(s) who gave you the information. Next, share the consolidated results with management for a reality check.

Working with Applications Development and Data Center Staff

Two other groups must be canvassed to complete the needs analysis. These include the Applications Development and Support Group and your data center staff. Though an integral part of IT, the Applications

Development and Support Group is a data center end user. In many cases, the applications groups are the primary interface between the data center and the business units. Applications development generally has the highest visibility and level of contact with the data center and much more consistent interaction with the business units. In most cases, the applications group is the data center's primary customer. Interview the applications development group in much the same way that you interview representatives of the business units.

Finally, you must consider operational and system management software needs. Operational initiatives are those technical and process components that the data center must maintain to run its operation. System management software is dictated by the technical architecture. You and your data center staff are the source of operational and system management requirements. But don't take for granted the inclusion of these needs. Be explicit. Meet with your staff to validate these needs before developing the final automation requirements.

▶ Automation Requirements

Automation requirements address the problems and opportunities that you identified in the "Before" picture. Once again, engage your staff. Schedule a work session to develop the solutions to the problem and opportunity statements. The solutions are stated as automation requirements for each technical and administrative process component. By now, the component and process list is familiar to them. And since they helped you develop the problem and opportunity statements, they have had some time to think about appropriate solutions.

Refer to Table 2–3 to develop an input model and output for this exercise.

Table 2–3 Automation Requirements

Component	Problem or Opportunity Statement	Requirements
Technical Architecture		
Performance Monitoring and Capacity Planning (PM/CP)	Only one threshold can be monitored per system resource	Ability to constantly monitor CPU average utilization
	Administration of monitoring schemes is spread out among systems and is manually intensive	Ability to set multilevel thresholds on CPU average utilization for automated alerting
	Reporting and trending is run and analyzed manually, which is time-consuming	Alerting scheme must provide and support multi-level auto-email and auto-paging for breech of threshold
		Ability to easily administer system components for additions, changes, and deletions
		Automated and configurable reporting on CPU usage: Weekly, monthly, and "year to date" usage Weekly and monthly predictive trend analysis for saturation
Process Architecture		
Change Management	Current administration (forms and submittal) is done manually, which is time-consuming	Ability to create and enhance form that technical staff will use to request changes to the production environment
	Current administration is prone to error and loss of work	Form must be submitted and stored in a database
	Current data is kept in file folders, which is not readily available and is often lost	Upon submittal of forms, system will provide an alert to responsible personnel for approval

Table 2–3   Automation Requirements *(continued)*

Component	Problem or Opportunity Statement	Requirements
		System will provide administrators email-style headings that will list requests by the following sorts and be easily configured for new sorts later: Open / In Process / Closed
		System will provide printing capabilities for forms and headings

Table 2–3 lists only the types of requirements that are defined for one technical and one process component. Details will vary from shop to shop, and the chart you develop will contain information that is customized to your environment.

▶ Validation of Automation Requirements vs. Needs Analysis

You have completed the development of automation requirements and validated them versus the problem and opportunity statements. Next, you need to review the user, application development, system management software, and operational needs (needs analysis) to validate that the new requirements support them or are at least neutral. If you identify conflicts, you will need to resolve them by changing or adding to the automation requirement(s). For example, assume that during your interviews with the application development group, you identified the need to monitor a database maintenance process that runs each weekend. And now that you are reconciling this against your monitoring automation requirements, you notice that you do not have a requirement that will cover monitoring the rebuilding of indexes, which is a key part of the database maintenance routine. This is an example of a disconnect between the automation requirements and user needs, which you caught through this step.

Alternatively, let's say that during your interviews with the user community, the requirement to have the application up and running ten hours a day, Monday through Saturday, was consistently communicated. This is an example of a user need that is not adversely affected by your automation requirements. That you gathered the requirements and confirmed that no changes were required is still important.

▶ The Gap

Let's review what you have developed so far, before proceeding to the last step in the gap identification process. Thus far, you have:

- Identified and documented the current automation level in your data center, and the problems and opportunities it represents.
- Identified and documented the end users' needs, applications development and support needs, and system management and operations needs.
- Developed a list of detailed automation requirements for both the technical and administrative process components of your data center.

Using this information, you will evaluate the new automation requirements versus current automation and describe the gap. Use the automation requirements matrix and expand it as you see in Table 2–4:

Table 2–4   Sample Gap Matrix

Component	Problem and Opportunity Statements	Automation Requirements	Currently in Place	The Gap/General Recommendations
Technical Architecture				
Performance Monitoring & Capacity Planning (PM/CP)	Only one threshold can be monitored per system resource	Ability to constantly monitor CPU average utilization	Full—through inherent OS utilities and monitoring scripts	Though currently provided, process is not well integrated into full PM/CP scheme
	Administration of monitoring schemes is spread out among systems and is manually intensive	Ability to set thresholds on CPU average utilization for automated alerting	Full—script intensive	Scripting maintenance is difficult to maintain
	Reporting and trending is run and analyzed manually, which is time-consuming	Alerting scheme must provide and support multi-level auto-email and auto-paging for breech of threshold	Partial—alerts are single level and must interact with paging software	Multilevel alerting & integrated/ single-product solution required
		Ability to easily administer multiple system components for additions, changes and deletions	No— administration is local to each machine— scripts are manually maintained	Full functionality required

Table 2–4   Sample Gap Matrix *(continued)*

Component	Problem and Opportunity Statements	Automation Requirements	Currently in Place	The Gap/General Recommendations
		Automated and configurable reporting on CPU usage:	No	Full functionality required
		Weekly, monthly, and "year to date" usage		
		Weekly and monthly predictive trend analysis for saturation		
Process Architecture				
Change Management	Current administration (forms and submittal) is done manually, which is time-consuming	Ability to create and enhance forms that technical staff will use to request changes to the production environment	Partial—current process uses word processor form	Though forms exist, they do not support the rest of this component's requirements
	Current administration is prone to error and loss of work	Form must be submitted and stored in a database	No	Full functionality required
	Current data is kept in file folders, which are not readily available and are often lost	Upon submittal of forms system will provide an alert to responsible personnel for approval	No	Full functionality required

Table 2–4   Sample Gap Matrix *(continued)*

Component	Problem and Opportunity Statements	Automation Requirements	Currently in Place	The Gap/General Recommendations
		System will provide administrators email-style headings that will list requests by the following sorts and be easily configured for new sorts later: Open / In Process / Closed	No	Full functionality required
		System will provide printing capabilities for forms and headings	No	Full functionality required

Using the same examples as in our *after* picture, we add two columns: "Currently in Place" and "The Gap/General Recommendations." The Gap/General Recommendations column simply states whether or not your current environment supports the specific requirement and provides a qualifier if appropriate. The "Gap/General Recommendations" column contains the conclusion of the analysis. The General Recommendations comments are important because, in addition to completing the gap equation, they also provide perspective. In the first example, the ability to constantly monitor CPU average utilization may not be enough to satisfy the requirements, as it is most likely not integrateable with the new functionality required and, therefore, may need to be replaced. The second example is even more extreme in that though a form is currently used, it cannot be used in a scheme that provides all the other newly defined functionality.

Upon completion of this chapter, you have a complete set of automation requirements that were derived from business users, applications development, and IT operations. You have engaged management and staff, both within and outside IT. Before you take on design and planning, you need to consider two key personnel issues: the impact of the automation project on the IT organization and your project staffing needs. These are addressed in Chapter Three.

3

The Organization

Having completed the exercises in Chapters One and Two, you have established realistic expectations for your automation initiative and a clear purpose statement to match. With input from your staff, users, and management, you diagnosed the problems and opportunities of automation in the *context* of your technology and process architectures. Now you need to assess the project in the *context* of your IT organizational structure and formally establish the team that will plan and execute the project.

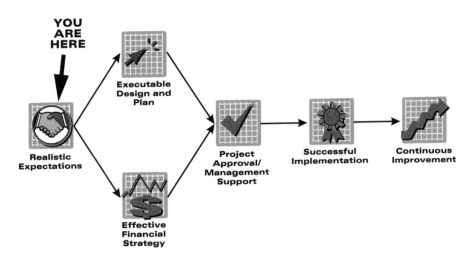

YOU ARE HERE

Realistic Expectations

Executable Design and Plan

Effective Financial Strategy

Project Approval/ Management Support

Successful Implementation

Continuous Improvement

A couple of years ago, I helped an insurance company address the organizational, process, and technology issues they faced as they were embarking on their first (perceived) distributed, client/server implementation. This company had been operating in legacy mode for over 30 years. The mainframe had been supporting their applications as long as they could remember, which was a long time, since most of the IT managers were "lifers" in the organization. They were quite anxious about the impending insurgence of the new UNIX- and Oracle-based technology, but they said nothing about the process and organizational implications. I suspected they could handle new technology; the real concern lay in their ability to change their processes and integrate new talent.

I used the term "perceived" in the preceding paragraph because the organization had been supporting a network for over a year. Novell and NT servers were up, running, and managed by a so-called "network group." The beleaguered network manager was the new hire in the organization, and his input and perspective were virtually dismissed by the incumbent legacy managers. The only time the incumbent operations manager worked with the "rookie" network manager was to resolve simple interface issues. In fact, the legacy managers built a wall to separate the mainframe from the network servers in the computer room. Talk about matching logical (attitudes) with physical (support)!

The physical and professional separation was a real shame for lots of reasons. In addition to the obvious relationship problems brought on by the "us against them" behavior, the lack of synergy did not permit the benefits of shared perspectives and experience, let alone joint problem-solving. The legacy operation was mature and stable but the newly established network group could not participate in the established, integrated production processes. Conversely, the network group brought the enterprise valuable technical knowledge but the legacy personnel weren't learning anything new. Every time the groups needed to work together, they ran headlong into a physical and attitudinal wall.

My initial directive-recommendation to the CIO? "Knock down that wall." We dealt with the organizational issues *first, and then built an integrated team to address the challenges of new technology.*

Whatever the project, managers must concern themselves with three critical aspects: people, process, and technology. In Chapters One and Two, the matrixes and exercises dealt with the technology and process architectures. The people issues were addressed in advice and tips about how to involve people in project definition by engaging them in evaluation of the opportunities and diagnosis of the problems. In every chapter, you will find advice and tips on how to engage, manage, and work with the people who will approve, execute, and experience change as a result of your automation project. These aspects of the automation project are interleaved in every subject and at every phase of the project and this book. This chapter contains a concentrated discussion of two "people" issues: first, how automation may impact the IT department's organizational structure, and second, how to establish an automation project team in the context of your IT department and enterprise.

This book is not focused on the structuring and restructuring of IT organizations, project management, or team building. However, your initiative is driven by and reliant on people. We need to stop and look at how your department is organized (why and what changes you might need to effect), and how to leverage that organization to build your automation team.

As you read this chapter and apply the ideas to your environment and challenges, expect to answer the following key questions:

- How am I organized compared to industry standards and norms?
- What management relationships outside Infrastructure/Operations should I be trying to nurture with respect to this initiative?
- For what typical organizational issues and challenges should I look?
- How should I compose and initiate an automation project team?
- What changes must I take on as part of this initiative?

▶ Prototype IT Organization

Start by understanding the high-level, direct-reporting structure to the senior IT official. The logic and history of your IT organizational reporting structure provide a useful basis for the analysis of organizational issues. Consider the prototype IT *functional* organization in Figure 3–1 and compare it to yours.

Note that the prototype is a *functional* organization. A functional organization chart highlights the major areas of operation or activity that compose a group—in this case, the IT department. The functional organization may not be directly aligned to the personnel organization chart, which contains names and titles arranged in a reporting structure (see Appendix B for a detailed Enterprise Services Personnel Chart). Utilizing both a personnel organization chart and a functional organization chart creates a distinction between the assignment of responsibility (personnel structure) and purpose (functional structure) within the organization.

The high-level organization chart that Figure 3–1 shows the functions that an IT executive is typically responsible for managing. Your personnel organization chart provides the context for the concepts in this chapter. Your reporting structure must account for all the functions illustrated in Figure 3–1. Let's examine each function more closely, and you'll see why.

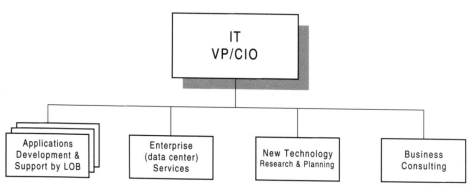

Figure 3–1   Prototype High-Level IT Functional Organization

Applications Development—
By Line of Business (LOB)

No matter what type of business is being supported (e.g., manufacturing, retail, etc.), application development (otherwise referred to as the insertion and maintenance of applications) is *managed* by LOB, even though the organizational structure and job titles may indicate otherwise. Examples of this include (a) the development director in the manufacturing business who has separated his staff's efforts among inventory, shop floor control, order entry, etc., and (b) a different manager in a similar business who has split his resources into initial development/deployment and ongoing maintenance/support. In larger organizations, you will find both a development organization that is split between development and support, and segmentation into subgroups organized by LOB. In other cases, lines of business are distinguished between internally developed and externally provided applications. In these cases, the two groups exercise similar methodologies with subtly different skill sets.

Whatever the organizational needs and specifics, the role of the Application Development function is to

> Lead the insertion of new and changing applications and maintain the stability of the software (only) throughout the life of the product.

The Applications Development professionals anticipate and react to the needs and requirements of the business units they support. With the possible exception of desktop support, the applications development group has the most visibility to the business or "end customer" in the enterprise. When business users are considering an application requirement to improve market penetration or responsiveness, they will call upon the Applications Development team for advice, support, and the development or evaluation of a solution.

Some authors would postulate that the most important success driver for the application development group is its ability to work with end users to develop requirements that make sense for the business within the limits of financial resources and technology. Few groups do it well, and we all suffer the consequences when development is based upon wrong or inadequate requirements. Equally important is the fact that the successful insertion of new or improved applications requires attention to the changes required by the enterprise to accept and use the new application. This aspect of "leading" is most often overlooked by applications development groups and by those who consult with them.

(New) Technology—Research and Planning

A typically overlooked, but critically important, responsibility of the CIO is the "Technology" function. All too often, decisions to insert new technologies and applications come from what I call "point-solutions." These decisions are made by application development and infrastructure managers—without respect to each other—at the last minute and without any strategic direction or standards. The result is a proliferation of non-standard technology, duplication of efforts, frustrated technical employees, and interdepartmental communications problems.

Savvy, budget-rich IT organizations generally have a Technology function to research and recommend new technologies geared toward driving the achievement of corporate business objectives. In some cases, the Chief Technology Officer has status and budget to rival his or her CIO counterpart. However, you don't have to have a Fortune-50 budget to put sufficient focus on this function. The role of the Technology function is to

> *Evaluate and recommend new technologies, and develop technical standards and guidelines that support the company's mission and business objectives.*

Context is critical in the effective Technology function. The company's financial performance, core strategies, business development objectives, and customer care orientation drive the recommendations developed by this function.

Business Consulting

What? In an IT organization? In today's marketplace, no IT organization can take the "business" from its internal users for granted. Better products and services at highly competitive rates are the name of the game. No IT organization is ensured that its services will be chosen by the business simply because they share the same corporate name. IT organizations must compete with outside sources. And guess what?

External competitors are marketing and selling. Most IT organizations, even the larger ones, have stopped short of naming an "IT Marketing Director," but many have created a business consulting function that

Actively markets and sells the services that the IT organization believes it provides as a competitive advantage for the business.

The IT business consultant meets regularly with the business units to promote the uses of information technologies in the context of business planning and the execution of strategies and tactics. As consultants to the user community, the personnel in these positions develop in-depth knowledge of the business. They make sure that users are getting the maximum benefits from the services and products provided by IT, and they help identify emerging needs and solutions early. In addition, they often report to the user community about the creation of new IT projects and the status of existing initiatives.

An IT group that does not have the budget to employ the "business consultant" should still view this as a critical function within the organization. In such cases, the CIO and/or his or her lieutenants (i.e., application development and operations directors) take responsibility for the function. The important thing is to recognize the function and give it the required resources and support.

Enterprise Services

Last, but not least, Enterprise Services is the operational foundation of the IT organization. Also known as "IT Operations" or "Infrastructure," the role of the Enterprise Services function is to

Build and maintain the stability of the environment that supports new and changing applications and the exchange of information in the enterprise.

Stability is achieved through sound process and technology architectures that meet production requirements derived from the requirements of the applications, end users, and IT personnel.

Since the Enterprise Services group will be the most affected by the automation initiative, let's take a detailed look at its structure in Figure 3–2.

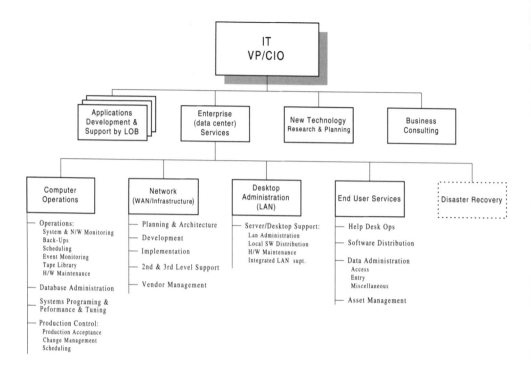

Figure 3–2 Prototype IT Functional Org – Enterprise Service Detail

This functional organization chart shows the general functions of the Enterprise or "operations" group in a "purist" arrangement. Be sure to note that it contains no reflection of technology, such as mainframe, UNIX, NT, etc.

You might look at this and think, "We're not organized like that because we're different. We're different because ours is a much smaller organization, or we have special needs that drive a different model, etc." If so, you are not alone. Many IT executives with established distributed platforms and operations have trouble relating to the model shown above and accepting it as a benchmark for restructuring their own organizations. In addition to the "we're different" syndrome, they resist the model for two primary reasons: first, it looks like a legacy organization, and second, their organization evolved to its current state in a series of iterations over time. As new technology was adopted, a new group was created to support it. Technology-based organizational structures come with problems that will be addressed in the next section of this chapter.

Whatever your size, industry, or corporate culture, I guarantee that the functions you see in the model above represent a core set of responsibilities that every enterprise services operation must manage. And to whatever extent possible, the most sensible approach is to organize and separate them in accordance with the model. Every enterprise must manage a data center environment, a wide area network infrastructure, a local area network environment that includes the desktop, and the end user services to manage the interface with the customer. The functions detailed in Figure 3–2 are the minimal set of responsibilities required to support these areas.

In Appendix B, Enterprise Data Center Services: Sample Organization and Management Job Descriptions contains a sample organization chart, complete with job titles. Also provided are sample job descriptions for management positions and purpose statements for staff positions. This material has been made available for those whose organization is not aligned with the functional organization chart and/or who are experiencing any of the typical problems listed below. Use the appendix as a reference in validating or refining your enterprise services organization.

▶ Typical Problems and Issues

In addition to comparing the way your operations group is organized versus the model above, let's discuss the typical problems you're likely to encounter while implementing your automation initiative. These three are the most prevalent that I've found in IT operations groups around the world:

1. Fragmentation.
2. Under-developed Process Infrastructure.
3. Operations functions in non-operations groups.

Fragmentation

Fragmentation is a huge issue for contemporary IT organizations. As explained above, the insertion of new technology has spawned the creation of separate technology groups within the same basic function.

This is most evident in—but not limited to—two areas: server and network administration. Examples of server administration fragmentation include the classic technology separation of powers between mainframe, UNIX, NT, etc. Each group works within its own silo. They don't communicate with each other and don't share production control processes required to keep the environment reliable and serviceable.

Network administration fragmentation is more often a product of geographical differences rather than technology. However, the impact is similar. What occurs is a lack of communications and well managed production processes required to keep the environment stable. If "the network is the data center," then how can support groups responsible for the same functions—within a different set of technical and geographical circumstances—support one enterprise effectively when they are fragmented?

Fragmentation also manifests itself in the problem management function, including Help Desk operations. The reasons for this occurrence are similar to server and network administration, where different processes exist for different groups, geographies, and technologies. The impact of this fragmentation causes user confusion—where to go for what and when—duplication of effort, and most importantly, difficulty in measuring and managing productivity.

The organization structure in Figure 3–2 eliminates the personnel and process fragmentation that occurs in organizations structured around their technologies. The people are aligned with the core functions that enterprise services must support, regardless of the technologies used to execute those functions.

Process Infrastructure

Typical "*process*" problems pick up where fragmentation issues leave off. As noted over and over again, production processes are not taken advantage of is fragmentation of responsibilities exists within the main enterprise services functions. In addition to fragmented support, much of the problem lies in the fact that no formal recognition, responsibility, and ownership exists for core production processes. These are the technical and administrative processes detailed as infrastructure components in Chapters One and Two. For example, change management is an established process existing in most, and I venture to say all, legacy environments. However, when dealing with the support of miscellaneous servers and networks in a fragmented manner, this process is not leveraged from or, in most cases, even duplicated. This means that core production processes are virtually ignored in many areas of an infrastructure that supports mission-critical business applications for your company.

"The network is the data center." No matter how "distributed" your contemporary enterprise has become, manage it as a single operation. I mentioned earlier that one of the problems IT executives had with my functional model is its "legacy feel." When it comes to managing the process infrastructure, consolidation is the most fail-safe strategy to ensure consistent utilization of processes.

Operations Functions in Non-Operations Group

One of the worst situations occurs when non-operational groups (i.e., application development) are managing operational functions. In short, the fox is guarding the hen house. Typically, this occurs when an applications development group has deployed a new system into production—often before it has been properly tested and accepted for production—and must lend their hands in stabilizing the system's environment by involving themselves in monitoring the system, schedule, and database. Though helpful in the short term, this group will have a hard time disengaging their first-line technical support and ongoing database administration over time. Remember that this situation came about because a sound production acceptance process was not enforced and/or followed.

The impact of this scenario is trouble, trouble, and more trouble. By nature, development groups will make continuous on-the-fly changes to code and the database. The application(s) will continually fail to operate as desired, as the quickly changing, unchecked operation doesn't allow you, the operations manager, to stabilize the environment.

Here are two symptoms to look for if you suspect that this situation plagues any one or more of your production systems:

1. Routine scheduling fixes are escalated to the Applications Development group as 1st-level support. In this scenario, opera-

tors and/or system administrators are not instructed or empowered to address anticipated and common operational problems.

2. The database administrator employed to architect, design, and develop the database is now playing ongoing operational administration.

If either of these two apply to any of your installations, you have an immediate organizational issue to escalate to the IT executive.

The Shared vs. Distributed Services Dilemma

Another common challenge you might be facing is the neverending question of shared versus distributed services. An age-old problem facing companies that rely on technology to support business operations derives from this question. The question struggled with is this: "where in the organization do certain, custom business-focused, rapid development personnel report?" Like many academic theories and practices in the marketplace, solutions have been applied in many different ways over time and then cycled through again and again, much like (yesterday's versus today's) clothing fashions—interesting how today's fashions resemble the 60's and 70's. So too has the dilemma of IT shared services versus dedicated resources.

For example, when distributed computing came to the forefront of the IT industry in the early 90's, the term "architect and distribute" was born. This was, in fact, a concept by which IT departments were to drive technology and standards and then stand back and let the front-line business units develop and manage their own custom development and support of systems and software in a self-dedicated manner. Today the trend has swung back to a more centralized development and support model, but not without its problems and issues.

Today, many IT organizations find themselves with both models and a hybrid. In some areas of the business, IT is responsible for managing shared services, such as the systems that run the company's financial tools. In other areas of the business, dedicated resources to develop and support software and systems are managed outside of IT. In many of these cases, development and support of single products are managed by both IT and non-IT resources.

The two main advantages to managing dedicated resources outside IT are:

1. Detailed knowledge of the business.
2. The ability to provide rapid development and deployment methodologies to solve specific, custom business needs.

Detailed knowledge of the business comes from living and reporting to the people for whom you are developing and deploying. The ability to provide rapid development stems from the detailed understanding of the business's needs, coupled with the fact that little bureaucracy is holding you back from providing quick, point solutions.

The disadvantages of this model are a bit more complex than the advantages and generally fall under the following three categories:

1. A disconnect between IT and the business.
2. The inability to support the products being developed in a cost-effective manner.
3. The inability to provide a high level of internal and external customer satisfaction.

The disconnect between IT and the business causes many problems. Although point solutions are being deployed in the business, they are just that, point solutions. They are often deployed without understanding of common technologies and processes that are important to the enterprise. Point solutions can cause problems in other areas of the technical environment simply because little or no coordination occurs between the appropriate groups. The results of all this cause:

- Reinvented wheels—wasted costs.
- Scarce IT resources within each business—the inability to pool resources.
- Lack of standards throughout the infrastructure—wasted costs and system integration problems.
- Too many technologies deployed that cannot be efficiently supported—wasted costs and frustrated personnel.
- Lack of reliability in the production environment—wasted costs and frustrated personnel.

- Confusion of roles and responsibilities between departments—wasted costs, duplication of efforts, and frustrated personnel.
- Miscommunication and resentments among personnel—frustrated personnel and poor morale.
- Increased costs for maintenance and upgrades to software to keep software in sync with changing business and technology.

No matter how much progress is made utilizing dedicated resources outside IT, these groups ultimately cannot fully support their tools in a production environment. Invariably, two things take place: production systems will attempt to be supported outside of the "production environment," and the dedicated resources will struggle with IT to support those things that have been deployed "in the production environment." The results? See the last six bullets above.

What do you do? Reign it in. Benefits achieved from the "pros" are being wiped out by the results suffered from the "cons."

If you suffer from these problems, I recommend that you consider the following two strategies to help address these issues:

1. Work with IT executive management to establish a formal, or to re-evaluate its existing, Systems/Business Analyst group. The responsibilities of this group should be to:

- Seek out and receive requests for information and/or development requirements.
- Analyze technical solutions to meet the requirements.
- Choose which internal and/or external resources will be utilized to fulfill the requirements.
- (Project) manage the initiative to fruition, ensuring the fulfillment of the solution.
- Once the solution is fulfilled, deliver the product to the customer.
- Provide a post-development customer care program (a process or set of processes required to continually analyze and respond to the needs, usability, and effectiveness of any given product).

The idea is to create an IT function that will act as the business units' super-users, providing the ability to provide rapid development stems from the detailed understanding of the business's needs. Also, you want to manage a centralized IT function that will follow and manage important IT processes, standards, communication, etc.

2. Identify all IT infrastructure functions currently being managed outside the department and move them into IT appropriately.

Automation Initiative—Staffing Issues

We've looked at the IT organization and, more specifically, its operations, the core functions, and the issues you are likely facing. How do these all apply directly to your automation initiative? The answer lies in the purity of the model. You must be very sure to consolidate fragmented groups, and initiate ownership and control of the production processes you have in place and those you need to insert.

A central focus of the automation initiative is the optimization of personnel. Later in this book, we address the specifics and expectations around this objective. Regardless of your expectations for personnel reductions, you need a well defined operation within each functional area and a cohesive team operating across functional areas for two reasons. First, this initiative has enterprise-wide impact. You will need central attention and focus from key technical support staff to help design, plan, and implement the project as an enterprise-wide solution. Second, once implemented, the new technical environment will require consolidated technical management.

As we discussed in Chapters One and Two, you will be automating several, if not all, of your infrastructure process components. If these processes are not fully implemented and/or are underrepresented, you will have a great deal of difficulty automating them. Reorganization and process implementation may very well be prerequisites to your automation initiative, and like the technical issues, require architecture, planning, and execution.

▶ High-level Functional Roles in the Automation Project

 Looking at the main IT functions and groups as described by their roles above, which should be considered as having a part in your automation initiative? The answer? Probably all of them. Figure 3–3 depicts a typical Automation Project Team structure.

Team Leader

Although this book is not a primer on project management or leadership, noting a few ideas on the key role of the team leader is worthwhile. Whether you perform this function yourself or delegate it to a trusted lieutenant, the leader will be responsible for:

- Project Initiation and Purpose Statement (Chapter One)
- Communications:
  The team leader must be vigilant to the need to keep all constituencies adequately informed. See the communications matrix in Chapter Six.
- Change Management:
  The team leader must develop and implement a process to manage changes to the project plan and work schedule.

  Note: This is not to be confused with business as usual, operational Change Management.

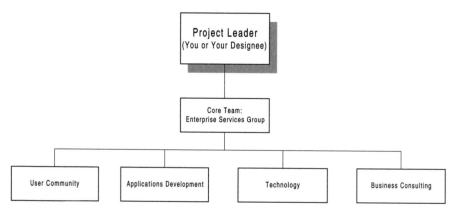

Figure 3–3 Project Team Organizational View

- Conflict Resolution and Ground Rules:
Conflicts will surface during the course of the project planning, design, and execution. The team leader should see to it that the team addresses conflicts. Conflicts must not be allowed to fester in hallway conversations. In addition, the team should develop explicit ground rules that will govern interactions among the team members, decision-making processes, and conflict resolution. Although all team members are responsible for supporting the ground rules, the team leader may need to issue reminders and mid-course corrections from time to time.

- Risk Management and Contingency Enactment:
The team leader must be ready to step up to the decisions required to enact contingencies, should they become necessary. Risk planning and the development of contingencies ahead of time will make this responsibility a little easier to fulfill (see Chapter Four).

Enterprise Services

The Enterprise Services group is the core team of the project. The core team is responsible for:

- Problem Diagnosis and Opportunity Assessment (Chapter Two).
- Planning and Design (Chapter Four).
- Inputs to the Financial Strategy (Chapter Five).
- Participation in the Project Approval Presentation (Chapter Six).
- Implementation and Continuous Improvement (Chapter Seven).

At a minimum, each of the functional areas in the Enterprise Services Group should be represented on the team. The representative should be a manager of sufficient standing to be able to command resources required for implementation.

In addition to the core team, which is drawn from the Enterprise Services Group, you will pull from the other functional areas in IT as well as the user community. The narrative below provides additional information concerning the roles of each.

Applications Development

The role of Applications Development in the automation initiative is critical. First, remember that the software technology this group inserts for the business drives your requirements. Their influence with the business and with the IT executive(s) makes their buy-in critical. Second, you are likely to need technical assistance from members of this group when deploying the technology that results from your automation planning efforts. Invite the manager of this group to project briefings. Copy him or her on status reports. And include applications development early in problem diagnosis, planning, and design.

The way you solicit and nurture their support is to communicate and focus them on the stability aspects of this initiative. Stability of the production environment supports stability in their products. Stability of their products makes them look good. Remember, since they are the primary interface to the user community, they are first in the line of fire when problems occur, even when the problems are infrastructure-based.

Technology

The Technology function will serve two roles. First, use your technology function as a source of information about new technologies and tools. Second, you may need their approval for the project to proceed. If your enterprise has a Technology function, its role is to evaluate and recommend new technologies. To the extent that you are taking the initiative in recommending an automation project, your technology director should be involved early. I suggest involving him or her in the exercises described in Chapter One. Take advantage of this valuable resource—you can't have a better champion or a more devastating adversary than your technology officer.

Business Consulting

If your organization fosters an IT Business Consulting function, tap in and use it. This organization knows how to talk to, sell to, and involve the enterprise in technology initiatives. Ask for advice and work with them to implement communications to the user community. They can help you develop the momentum to get your project approved, funded, and implemented.

User Community

The user community needs to know that IT is undertaking an automation initiative. They play a role in needs analysis, but most importantly, they need to understand enough about the project and its long-term benefits to support the effort and understand any of the disruptions that might come about during implementation and fine-tuning.

Context is critical to evaluate who needs to be informed and when. Maybe the personnel you interview to complete your needs analysis are the ones who need to receive project updates and briefings from time to time, or at least a high-level schedule and milestones along with the project purpose.

You have successfully engaged the user community if:

1. they know about the project and why it is being undertaken,
2. they believe that those users who should provide input were given the opportunity to do so, and
3. they support the objectives enough to put up with a little inconvenience along the way, if necessary.

In closing, this chapter highlights some of the fundamental aspects of assessing the people issues that arise in the management and execution of your automation project. These fundamentals include, first, understanding the IT organization and the impact of the automation project on the functions and structure of your IT department, and second, understanding how to draw upon the structure and organization to build an automation project team. Now you are ready to work with your team on additional planning and design.

Design and Planning

You have established realistic expectations for your automation initiative and assessed your project in Chapters One and Two. By completing Chapter Three, you developed a preliminary assessment of the organizational implications and you identified and established your project team. You are now ready to design the solution and prepare an executable plan. Note that you could be developing the financial plan (Chapter Five) at the same time:

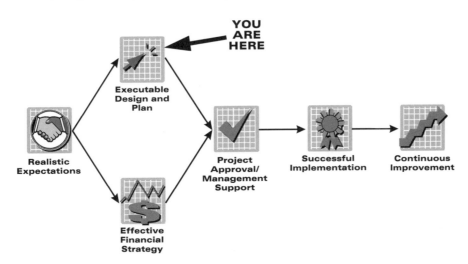

Time and time again, I have been brought into a data center operation after an unsuccessful deployment due to little or no design and planning. In case after case, managers start with technology—the latest widget to solve their problems—and end up worse off. They buy the "solution" without proper evaluation, analysis, design, planning, and buy-in. The results are devastating: low morale, missed deadlines, wasted money, damaged relationships, and technical performance that is the same or worse than before the installation. This book is heavily front-loaded with information on all the aspects of project setup and planning. In fact, six of the seven chapters address the people, process, and technology issues that must be addressed before deployment. If you don't have time to scope, design, and plan your automation project, you surely don't have time to deal with the problems you'll create during implementation. Careful design and planning will reward you with an easier implementation—not necessarily without its challenges—but manageable overall.

This chapter describes an approach to the design and planning aspects of the automation initiative. The design work encompasses two equally important and parallel activities: 1) evaluating and choosing the system management software to support the technology architecture components and 2) defining or refining the administrative processes and choosing the technology to support them. These two design activities may be executed simultaneously and do not depend upon each other. The consolidated design is composed of the system management software, redesigned administrative processes, and the tools to support them.

Planning refers to the development of the project plan, which may overlap with design but cannot be finished until the design is complete. This chapter does not contain a primer on project planning and project management. It does highlight the particular nuances of project planning in the context of automation initiatives.

As you read this chapter and apply the ideas and exercises to your environment and challenges, expect to fully qualify and answer the following key questions:

- Of what is the consolidated design composed?
- How do I make decisions regarding outsourcing vs. insourcing, and what aspects are most suitable for each?

- How do I organize the work?
- What are the special considerations in project planning for an automation initiative?

▶ Designing the Technical Architecture and Administrative Processes

As presented in the introduction to this chapter, the design work for the automation of technology architecture and administrative processes occurs separately and simultaneously. The first step in the design process is to split your effort into the "technical and process" categories identified in the first chapter. (You'll recall that you have ten technical architecture components and five technical or administrative process components.) The split is logical and desirable because the work can be executed simultaneously and you have no dependencies to track, although you do have interfaces. For example, increasing capacity due to the result of Performance Monitoring/Capacity Planning (a technical architecture component) will trigger the change management process (an administrative process). But the planning and design can and should be undertaken in two tracks: technical architecture and administrative processes. Take advantage of these characteristics by assigning the design activities to two different managers, who will work with different staff, vendors, and products. If this approach is not possible due to resource restrictions, you may want to consider executing the projects linearly, giving up the parallel advantage the split offers you.

Technical Architecture Design

Let's start with designing the automation of the technology architecture. The design phase should be assigned to a project manager. Assess the size of your department and the combination of the talent and availability of your qualified staff. The technology design project manager should assemble a team of experts who will participate in the solution development and design process.

The technical solution will result in system management software solutions that have implications for system, storage, and peripheral hardware; network hardware and software; and database software as depicted in Figure 4–1:

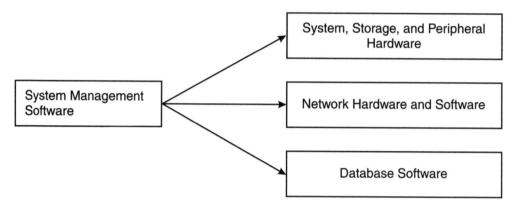

Figure 4–1 Technical Solution

The design process is fairly simple and straightforward. Use the auto-mation requirements to develop a request for proposals. Issue the request to external vendors and to your own staff. Receive and evalu-ate the responses and choose the solution that most closely meets your automation requirements. The solution may be purchased from an out-side vendor, developed internally, or created by a combination of inter-nal and external resources. This process is depicted in Figure 4–2.

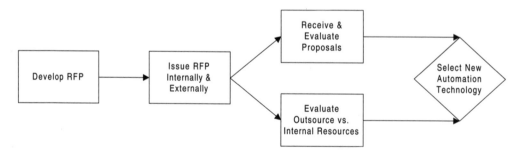

Figure 4–2 Technology Design Process

Related Selection Criteria

A great deal has been written about methodologies for evaluating pro-posals from developing and issuing Requests for Proposals (RFPs), cre-ating selection criteria, evaluating the responses, and engaging key staff and decision makers in the evaluation. These methodologies and approaches are outside the scope of this chapter. However, certain key considerations and related selection criteria are germane to automation initiatives. These are briefly summarized in the next three sections.

Platform Architecture

The platform architecture requirements are an important consideration, because features such as supportability and cost will have substantial impact on system management software and the automation of operations. Additionally, platform architecture requirements will be the most expensive to fulfill.

Supportability in this context means skill set investment. For example, if you have a substantial investment in Oracle database talent, you would not want—simply for reasons of feature functionality—to insert Sybase as a new database platform or vice versa. The required training and new talent would be too costly and the technical issues too complex, ultimately distracting from your core initiative.

However, however, however, and I mention this cautiously, you may have an opportunity to make a change in a platform you've been wanting to change. In other words, you may choose to take advantage of the initiative to achieve related objectives that are not within the scope of the automation project. For example, this project might be your opportunity to migrate from a single-vendor server/hardware solution to a multi-vendor scheme or vice versa. Whatever your appetite, be careful that your focus on the primary objective, automation, does not get defused or undermined by auxiliary efforts.

Budget

Although the budget isn't developed yet, the responses to the RFP will contain cost estimates. These quotes can be used to help develop the final budget and to eliminate responses that are wildly out of line—low or high. Before you eliminate a proposal, be sure to validate that the respondent's cost structure and components are an apples-to-apples comparison to the other proposals. If you are particularly attracted to a proposal that is a cost out-lyer, validate the information with the supplier and/or offer them the opportunity to re-bid.

Timeline

Your project plan will contain milestones and dependencies, but it is being developed concurrently with your technical solution. For purposes of evaluating RFP responses, timing issues include items such as budget cycles, execution of related projects, the pressure to upgrade related technology to increase space, scaleability, etc. If the timeline for the initiative is pre-ordained, include it in the RFP.

Identifying Vendor and Outsourcing Opportunities

Outsourcing is an ongoing consideration in data center operations. As you prepare the technical architecture design and eventually the financial plan (Chapter Five), you will need to analyze the cost effectiveness of outsourcing the product(s), implementation of the project, and/or ongoing service. Deciding what to outsource, when to outsource, and how to manage outsourced talent is both complex and challenging, so much so that dozens of articles and books are written on the subject. This section contains some basic considerations for outsourcing decisions in the context of designing the technical architecture. These concepts will also apply to the development of the financial case for your initiative and to the design for automation of the administrative process components.

Automation projects offer three general opportunities for outsourcing consideration:

- Product
- Implementation
- Ongoing Service

Software Product - Build versus Buy

When you completed the exercises described in Chapters One and Two, you identified which components of your data center operation were candidates for automation. Automation of any of the technical architecture components will require a decision regarding the use of third-party software products vs. building the functionality in-house. Basically, you have three options; one, purchase a third-party software product and use it "as is"; two, purchase a third-party software product and have it customized to meet your requirements; or three, build the functionality yourself.

Purchasing the Software

You can expect to invest the most time and money on outside resources in the purchase, customization, and ongoing support of your system management software. Companies and personnel in general accept the fact that in most cases, third-party, "off the shelf" products are preferable to re-creating the wheel. An extreme example of this includes office automation tools, such as the Microsoft® Office suite, which in spite of its faults enjoys a nearly universal install base. Why would any company, even one whose core competency is software development, want to develop its own suite to replace the functionality that Microsoft Office provides? The same logic may apply to the system management tools that you will consider using to automate the technical components.

Assuming that you have made the decision to purchase third-party software, you'll then need to decide how much, if any, customization is required. First you must identify which software product most fully meets your requirements. A decision must be made whether or not the product meets a sufficient number of your requirements or whether customization is required to bring the installation to the desired level of functionality. At this point, you should leverage the expertise of your potential vendor. Put him/her to work to provide you with the scope of the development and related costs so that you have qualified information for your implementation and financial plans. Later you can use these projections to compare the vendor's costs and time factors to your cost and time to provide the same customization internally.

Building Your Own Product

The decision to build your own functionality may not be self-evident, depending on the size and complexity of your initiative, your functional requirements, and your budget. Two types of system management tools exist: specific performance and capacity utilities, and full-blown enterprise management tools.

If your requirements are pointing you toward enterprise-sized system management products, you typically have no reason to consider building your own. The requirement set is too large. In fact, installations of products this size generally require a vendor-assisted custom implementation that can become a significant development project on its own.

The most attractive option you will have for building your own system management tool will be in specific performance and capacity utilities. To drill down further, consider monitoring and alerting functions. Many of the hardware products you have or are considering have utilities you can leverage from and interface to. These include inherent operating system and database utilities.

Let's take a look at some examples of how operating system and database utilities can be used. Suppose that you've identified Disk Capacity Management—low to medium complexity—and a set of specific requirements call for automated notification at different levels when a disk reaches certain thresholds as shown in Table 4–1.

Table 4–1 Sample Disk Capacity Management Requirements

Monitored Component	Threshold	Notification Scheme	Recipients
System Disks (physical volumes) & Logical Partitions	90%	Email	System Administration
	95%	Auto-Page	System Administration
	98%	Auto-Page	System Administration
			Data Center Mgmt.
Application Disks (physical volumes) & Logical Partitions	85%	Email	System Administration
	90%	Auto-Page	System Administration
	95%	Auto-Page	System Administration
			Data Center Mgmt.
Data Disks (physical volumes) & Logical Partitions	75%	Email	System Administration
	80%	Auto-Page	System Administration
	85%	Auto-Page	System Administration
			Data Center Mgmt.

From a low-complexity standpoint, these requirements are easily addressed by choosing from multiple system and subsystem utilities. For instance, for internal system disks, inherent UNIX OS commands and scripting can be set up in the cron-tab to run periodically and poll the disks. After a threshold is reached, the script responds with email and/or paging as configured. For external disk units, storage subsystem volume management software can be configured to provide the same service.

However, if you want to manage more than one platform architecture component from one technical solution, your low-complexity project will increase in complexity and cost. To keep cost and complexity low, consider managing each platform architecture component with a dedicated system management tool (perhaps one you build internally). In these cases, your cost factors will include what I refer to as "soft cost," which is basically the cost of the time and the use of staff hours you already have available.

Soft costs affect personnel management and the human resource component of the departmental budget allocated to the fulfillment of your projected core functions. When considering budget issues that affect personnel required to fulfill your in-house automation requirements, consider both the time required to build the technical schemes and the time required to support and maintain them. Support and maintenance requirements include fixing the schemes when they break and keeping them current to the ever-changing configuration of the system(s) they manage. The choices you make about using multiple system management tools will affect both your financial plan and project plan directly.

Administrative Process Components

Designing the automation of administrative processes is often overlooked. It involves more than the purchase of new tools. It requires taking an inventory of existing processes and refining them to support the new levels of automation delivered by the tools. The redesign of administrative processes and training to accept the new procedures is the most frequently overlooked activity in automation projects. Yet without this work, the entire initiative can fail. In fact, its omission is the most common cause of failure. I cannot stress the importance of the task enough.

In addition, administrative process design is more complicated, demanding, and time-consuming than choosing the system management software. Though one system management software suite could be used to address the automation needs of the technology architecture components, no single, pre-designed tool suite is available today to support the automation of the five administrative processes. The processes themselves can be more fully automated, reducing the need for manual procedures. So all steps of the design process must be executed for each administrative process.

Choosing a project manager for this activity is tricky. The ideal candidate would be a seasoned production control specialist with good communications skills, and basic system administration and technical data center knowledge. This person is your "production process architect" and will champion the effort. I use the word *architect* deliberately. The point is that an effort to digitize and automate your process infrastructure will require you to construct or reconstruct the way you do business. In addition, a whole, self-contained methodology and discipline is at work in the architecture of infrastructure processes for distributed production environments. Refer to the Enterprise series, *Rightsizing the New Enterprise, Managing the New Enterprise, Networking the New Enterprise,* and *Building the New Enterprise,* authored by Harris Kern, for more information.

So that you don't have to keep flipping back to Chapter One, here is the list of production process components and their descriptions that you have considered for better automation:

- Production Acceptance—*Process that identifies the operational requirements to implement and manage new and changing applications*
- Problem Management—*A centralized process to manage and resolve user network, application, and system problems*
- Change Management—*A process that coordinates all changes that affect the production environment*
- Asset Management—*Process to query, discover, track, and store enterprise computing resources, including hardware, operating systems, and applications*
- Disaster Recovery—*Process to enable recovery in the event that a disaster should render mission-critical systems inoperable*

Figure 4–3   Administrative Process Reengineering and Technical Design

Note that you may have processes similar to the ones named above, but you may associate them with different titles and terminology. In some cases, you may have matching processes that are un-named. This situation is no problem, because you will recognize the processes here and be able to easily map them back to your system.

The design process is depicted in Figure 4–3.

You have developed automation requirements for the administrative processes as part of the "after" picture. Next, you need to validate that you have well designed and defined processes in place. To do so, you will validate or refine them versus the standards that I have provided in Figure 4–3. If your processes don't look like the standards I have provided, you have problems. Adopt the standard and document the differences between how you are executing today and how you should be executing. Use your new (or validated) process objectives and definitions to validate that your automation requirements are both necessary and appropriate. Then use the validated requirements to develop and issue an RFP for the technical solution set. Select the solution set. Your final administrative process design will have two components: revised or validated process definitions/objectives and the technical solution set.

The next several pages of this chapter provide the information you need to validate or redesign your processes to meet performance-proven standards. Again, I cannot emphasize the importance of this work enough. Study this material and apply it carefully. If you do not provide for the process redesign and training, your initiative will surely fail.

Document and Audit Existing Processes

Start by documenting and auditing each of your administrative processes as you execute them today. The sections below contain a standard for the objectives and definitions of the administrative processes, Production Acceptance, Problem Management, Change Management,

Asset Management, and Disaster Recovery. In most cases, your processes should match up with these standards; if not, you will need to revise them. Once again, engage your staff in this exercise. You will need to document revisions thoroughly to prepare for the training and implementation required to adopt the new or revised process in the deployment (Chapter Seven).

Production Acceptance Objective and Process

The Production Acceptance process is used to identify deployment and ongoing operational requirements for new and enhanced applications. Its objective and process are as follows:

Objective:

To establish and maintain a process to identify the operational requirements to deploy and provide ongoing support to new distributed applications in the production environment.

This is established by identifying the technology of new applications in their early phases of concept and architecture. Groups responsible for the deployment of the application platform and ongoing operations can better ready themselves by profiling the application early on.

- Communicating roles and responsibilities
- Communicating processes between groups

Process:

The Production Acceptance process for any given application, system, or project is initiated by a "Project Lead." Anyone responsible for introducing a new concept into the production environment may be the Lead: a software developer, end users, business analyst, etc.

A Production Acceptance team manages this process, led by a coordinator. The team is made up of representatives from the following operational functions:

- NW Operations
- Systems and Database Management

- Help Desk
- Computer Operations
- Production Control (usually plays the role of the "Coordinator")

The process incorporates periodic team meetings that present, track, and close out the following:

- New IS initiatives being introduced
- Progress on initiatives in process
    - Open Issues
    - Milestones
    - Progress
    - Sign-Off

This team will work up front with Application Developers and users to understand the requirements necessary to implement and support a distributed application. The team will act as consultants to guide the customers to a successful and expedient system implementation. The process flows as shown in Figure 4–4.

Figure 4–4 shows that a new or enhanced system, application, or project is introduced in this process at the point of conception. A questionnaire is then filled out, outlining the description and requirements of the system being introduced. Those requirements are worked on by the various operational support groups and are readied for sign off.

Note that operational support groups responsible for implementation are charged with moving their piece of the project forward into production. This includes their areas of change management.

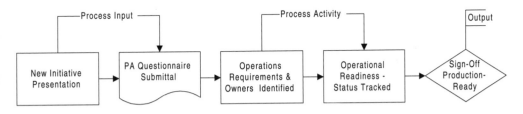

Figure 4–4 Production Acceptance Process Flow

Problem Management Objective and Process

Problem Management is much more than a help desk tool, rather it is the process by which the tools support a proactive, as well as reactive, way of identifying, logging, tracking, and ultimately resolving problems. Its objective and process are as follows:

Objective:

The objective of the problem management scheme is to track and resolve problems expediently using a disciplined problem management system, including tools, and guidelines in order to:

- Establish an ongoing process of resolving problems
- Minimize their impact on IT services
- Optimize the time and effort spent in problem solving

Note that this objective includes and is very often focused on internal data center tracking that includes proactive and automatic notification to the problem management system for resolution.

Process:

The problem management process flow (pictured in Figure 4–5) includes:

- **Problem recognition**—detection and identification of problems or potential problems, through monitoring, observation, and/or trend analysis.
- **Problem reporting/logging**—central notification of the occurrence of a detected problem and recorded information for subsequent handling.
- **Problem determination and identification** of the source of a problem at a level sufficient to enable corrective action.
- **Bypass/Recovery**—a partial or complete circumvention of a problem, usually prior to final resolution.
- **Problem Resolution**—the final corrective action that repairs, replaces, or modifies the source of a problem.

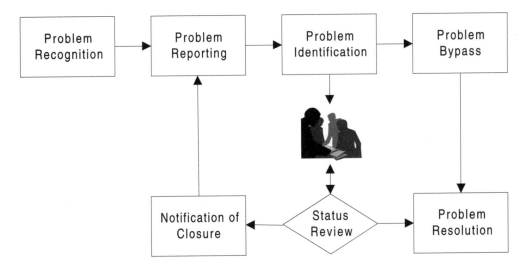

Figure 4–5 Problem Management Process Flow

- **Management Review**—management evaluation and control of overall operation and achievement of the problem control process.

Although the purpose of the Problem Management system is to manage the flow of problems to ensure organizational efficiency and effectiveness, the ultimate goal is to get the problems solved and eliminate each as a potential or actual outage. To accomplish this, an organization must rely on a Problem Coordinator. Responsibilities of the Problem Coordinator include:

- Overseeing the problem management system
- Tracking problem activities from open to close
- Invoking escalation procedures
- Monitoring reassignments for problem determination and resolution
- Utilizing and analyzing reports
- Chairing Problem Management Review meetings
- Presenting recommendations to management

Problem Coordinator responsibilities can be held or shared by any one of the following functions:

- Customer Service/Help Desk Manager
- Production Control (staff or management)
- Operations Manager
- IS Project Manager (staff)

Problem status review meetings are to be held on an ongoing basis to review current availability and stability attainment and outage analysis. Problems in exception status, including a review of their action plans and severity levels, will be examined and escalated as appropriate. This meeting should take no longer than half an hour. Attendees: Data Center Management, Problem Coordinator, and others as required. Representatives at these meetings have the responsibility for communicating any issues related to their specific areas of accountability.

Change Management Objective and Process

Change Management is the dynamic process that ensures day-to-day activities within the current production environment and maintains stability within that environment. Its objective and process are as follows:

Objective:

To establish and maintain a process for the review, documentation, and authorization of changes to the computing system prior to implementation. And to control the impact of "required" changes, reducing problems, and improving the probability of achieving reliable, available, and serviceable-disciplined computing objectives, including:

- Application changes
- Data file changes
- Hardware upgrades
- Operating systems and middleware changes
- Bug fixes
- New applications affecting dependencies

Figure 4–6 Change Management Process Flow

Process:

The process flow for Change Management is based on a fairly simple set of steps (see Figure 4–6):

- **Request**—Requester solicits the change
- **Approval**—A predetermined approval chain gives its consent
- **Communication**—Scheduled change is communicated to the support and user communities
- **Change**—The change is made or attempted by the responsible party and documented
- **Status**—The responsible party for the change communicates the status after the change was attempted

The requester communicates changes to production control, who is responsible to turn the request around in a predetermined amount of time (service level). Owner routes the form to members of the approval chain identified in the form for approval.

Owner then enters the change in a weekly-published Change Control Report, notifying all affected personnel of changes pending.

Responsible person makes the change and subsequently submits a status report to Production Control, who then logs and adds to the next weekly report (which contains a "status" section) and files.

Emergency Change Control

Senior operations executive management should be identified and granted authority to approve emergency changes. This involves calling or paging the person with Production Control responsibilities, help desk, or other appropriate means, with the emergency. Production Control will contact senior operations staff for authorization to proceed. If approval is given, the change is made. Production Control will then communicate, log, and file.

Asset Management Objective and Process

Asset Management is the scheme that combines procurement of IT hardware and software assets with the process to log, track, and report on, providing an end-of-life path to those assets. Its objective and process are as follows:

Objective:

To establish and maintain a process that ensures the effective and accurate input, update, retrievability, and auditability of IT computing resources. And to establish an end-of-life (EOL) process to systematically identify assets that have aged off the books and are no longer useful to the enterprise and to cycle them out of the environment.

Process:

This process manages assets as requested by the owner of the assets. Data is gathered and maintained on each asset. The data is entered and the tools manage and maintain the data on a going-forward basis. Assets being managed require an end of life process. Requirements for this process are determined and implemented by the asset management owner.

Changes and updates to the production environment are tracked by the Change Management system, as it will document and track the status of those changes. Changes to non-production elements defined as assets to be tracked, such as desktop units, will have to be updated in a more manual fashion. The overall flow of asset management will resemble Figure 4–7.

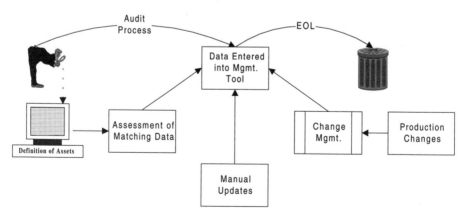

Figure 4–7   Asset Management Process Flow

Disaster Recovery Objective and Process

Disaster Recovery is the plan, process, and resources required to recover should a disaster render your operation inoperable. Its objective and process are as follows:

Objective:

To establish a plan and practice a process for recovering mission-critical applications based on business risk and priorities.

Process:

The process to implement Disaster Recovery begins with the plan. The plan is based on the concept of the Production Recovery Facility (PRF), containing all the hardware and network connections required to function as a data center. The plan assumes the following:

- Regular tape backups of the UNIX filesystems and databases on the critical production servers are being created and maintained.
- Backup tapes are being stored at an off-site storage facility. These tapes are available and undamaged.
- A procedure is in place to get the backup tapes from the off-site storage facility to the recovery center.
- Required personnel and transportation are available to staff the recovery center.

At recovery time, the designated servers in the PRF will be booted and restored from the backup tapes of the primary servers. The goal is to have the backup server come up and appear to the rest of the network as if the primary server had just been booted, with no changes needed to any client machine anywhere on the network. This can be accomplished through replication.

As part of the process of restoring the primary servers, the names of the backup servers will be changed to the names of the primary servers. However, the IP addresses of the backup servers will not be changed (keeping their original IP addresses).

As part of the recovery process, the Domain Name Service (DNS) and Network Information Service (NIS) tables must be updated to reflect the new mapping between machine names and IP addresses.

Once formal declaration of a disaster has been made, the following activities begin:

- Restore the business-processing environment

The off-site data storage vendor will be notified to ship the backup tapes to the PRF. As soon as the tapes arrive, restoration of the operating environment will begin.

- Run production from the PRF

Once the business-processing environment has been restored, production operation will begin. Full production processing will be available, but development activity may be restricted.

- Prepare for leaving the PRF

Depending on the extent of damage to the main data center, three options will be available:

1. Repair and reoccupy the data center
2. Obtain a replacement facility
3. Change the PRF to a data center

As soon as the operating environment is restored in the PRF and production is under way, a team will be selected and work will begin to implement one of these options.

Administrative Process Design Review

By way of review, the purpose of validating that the processes you have in place meet industry standards is to identify what must change to take full advantage of the automation tools you intend to purchase or create. These changes will affect the planning and subsequent deployment of your automation initiative. With input from your staff, you have recreated or enhanced your process descriptions using what you have learned from validating the process objectives, reviewing the process definitions, and factoring in the automation requirements. You now have a redesigned process and are ready for the evaluation and selection of the technology to support a new level of automation for each one (see Figure 4–8).

```
┌──────────────┐     ┌──────────────┐     ┌──────────────┐     ┌──────────────┐
│ Admin. Process│    │ Validate or Revise│ │ Validate Automation│ │ Develop &    │     ╱╲
│ Component &   │──▶ │ Current Process│──▶ │ Requirements vs.│──▶ │ Issue RFP /  │──▶ ╱Redesigned╲
│ Related Auto- │    │ Ojectives & Definition│ │ Process Objectives &│ │ Select      │    ╲Process & Related╱
│ Requirements  │    │ to Meet Standards│   │ Defiinition  │     │ Technical    │     ╲Automation╱
└──────────────┘     └──────────────┘     └──────────────┘     │ Solution Set │      ╲Technology╱
                                                                └──────────────┘       ╲╱
```

Figure 4–8 Administrative Process Reengineering and Technical Design

Use the validated automation requirements to develop a request for proposals. Issue the request to external vendors and to your own staff.
Receive and evaluate the responses and choose the solution that most
closely meets your automation requirements. The solution may be purchased from an outside vendor, developed internally, or created by a
combination of internal and external resources. Does this seem familiar?
It should. You are following the same process that is used to evaluate
and select the system management software solution. Note that the budget, timeline, and outsourcing considerations described within the technology architecture design section above apply to the selection of
technical tool sets to support the automation of administrative processes.

Consolidated Design

Upon completion of the design, you will have chosen a system management software suite provided by a vendor, internal resources, or some
combination of the two. You will have completed the redesign or validation of your administrative processes and will have chosen the technology to support their automation. You are now ready to turn your
attention to the plan.

▶ Planning—Highlighting Automation Project Nuances

This chapter does not contain a primer on project planning and management. However, by way of review, your project plan should contain
the following components at a minimum:

- **Tasks:** steps required to deliver the milestone.

- **Timeline**: deadlines associated with tasks and milestones.
- **Dependencies**: sequencing and relationship between milestones and tasks.
- **Risks and Contingencies**: identification of risks and mitigating factors.
- **Resource Allocations**: staff requirements and time required to complete tasks.
- **Budget**: cost of the project, including staffing, product purchasing, deployment, administration, etc.

In general, the table of contents of this book is a good structure for the project plan. Specific content will change based on the variables addressed in this book and the nuances of your environment and objectives. For example, working with 20 servers, as opposed to one, will increase the dependencies and risk factors you will consider. Nonetheless, the structure for the plan should mirror the methodology described in this book. In short, the components of your plan (tasks, milestones, resources, etc.) should map to the major steps outlined in the various chapters:

Plan Outline	Chapter Reference
Opportunity/Problem Definition	Chapter One
Scope of Work	Chapter Two
Organizational Impacts	Chapter Three
Design	Chapter Four
Financial Planning and Budgeting	Chapter Five
Communications	Chapter Six
Deployment	Chapter Seven
Continuous Improvement	Chapter Seven

Planning the Automation Initiative

The primary purpose of this section is to highlight the particular differences and levels of effort between the technical automation project and the work to execute the administrative process enhancement and its supporting technology. You'll recall that I recommend splitting the design into two parts: technical architecture design and administrative process design. Similarly, split the implementation activity into the same categories. Implementation is dealt with in Chapter Seven: Deployment and Continuous Improvement. The following mock project plan (see Figure 4–9), containing the technical automation and administrative process enhancement and its supporting technology efforts, illustrates the split in the context of the design work.

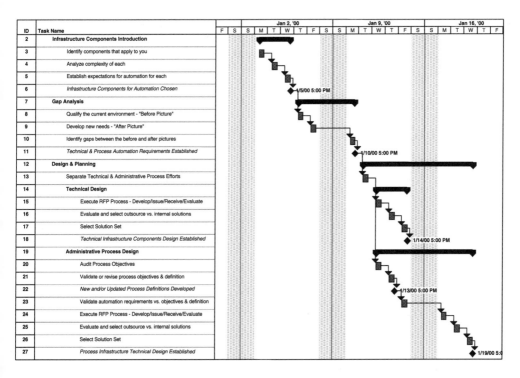

Figure 4–9   Sample Automation Project Plan

Notice that the overall tasks and milestones match the methodology you have been following throughout this book. More importantly, notice the differences and the similarities between the design work for the respective technical and administrative process components. First the differences:

Once the requirements are defined for the technical components, you will move quickly into the RFP and selection process.

However, the steps to move forward with the administrative process components after the technical requirements have been captured in the Gap Analysis are much more complex, requiring you to audit, validate, and perhaps consider revising your current processes.

Now, the similarities: both processes follow the same RFP and selection process. Choosing the solution set for the administrative process components requires following the same steps required to choose the system management software to automate the technical component. Chapter Seven will examine how the implementation activities are split in Deployment.

5

Financial Planning

Using the results of your gap analysis and some of the outputs of the design work, you can create a financial strategy to support the investment in automation. The financial planning work occurs in parallel with the design and planning activities described in Chapter Four:

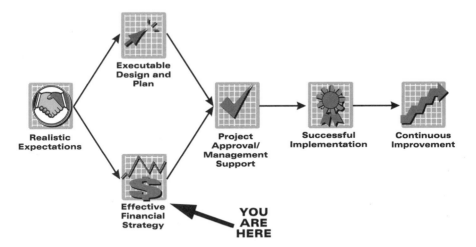

The network components of the data center and the advent of the Internet deliver greater access to information for a broader scope of users than ever before. This connectivity has created endless automation and remote system management possibilities. Whenever I'm asked whether any given

initiative can be accomplished, the answer is always a resounding "yes," immediately followed by the question, "How much time and money do you have?"

This chapter addresses the investment equation. In it, you will find the information, tools, and exercises to answer the following questions:

- What are the pros and cons of lease vs. buy?
- What are the key considerations in outsourcing ongoing service(s)?
- How do I develop the business case required to help sell the final plan to upper management?

IT executives and managers are well aware of budgetary constraints. They manage spending and financing considerations daily. Now that you've identified your requirements and developed your automation design and plan, you have the data you need to address two key issues in succession: (a) ownership, which includes lease versus buy and what vendor outsourcing solutions are available and applicable, and (b) the cost benefit analysis, which answers the question, "Can the costs be justified?"

▶ Ownership

Ownership is a key issue. The relevant question is "how many of the components in my technical plan can and/or should I contract to the vendor?" The areas to consider when answering this question include hardware leasing and ongoing service.

Choosing Lease versus Buy

Frequently, lease versus buy is a predetermined company-cultural decision. Accounting rules and the way your company has adopted them are likely to dictate the lease versus buy decision. Heavily leveraged companies that stress capitalization may require the purchase of hardware so that other costs such as expenses related to implementation can be included in depreciation.

Whatever your company's culture or purchasing policy, make sure that you understand and consider it in your financial plan and cost benefit analysis. If you don't know what your purchasing policies are, find out from finance and/or your IT executive. If you think you do, validate your assumptions with your finance department and IT executive. Failure to comply with cultural and purchasing norms could result in exhaustive rework after you've submitted your case to upper management, unless you address and justify your deviation from the norm. For example, if you work for a company that typically purchases and capitalizes hardware, you may have a shortage of cash in your current fiscal period. In spite of the existing company purchasing policy, a lease option may make sense to upper management and the concept could be well received. In some cases, the lease option will be the only way to get your initiative approved.

Leasing Benefits

Leasing can offer several attractive benefits, especially when cash-budget constraints are tight. These include:

- Low initial cash layout
- Ability to finance service costs
- Upgrade path to future hardware

Leasing will positively affect the department's bottom line (vs. purchasing), especially if the lease term begins in the latter half of your fiscal year. The amounts billed will include only the initiation fees, monthly payments, and finance charges. While you're at it, consider integrating maintenance and other service costs directly related to the hardware. Incorporation of ancillary expenses in the monthly payment provides two additional benefits. First, the costs are spread out over the life of the lease, and second, you don't have to track or pay for these costs separately. Leasing can also offer you an attractive way to package and sell the inevitable upgrade of hardware later on. Structured correctly, the lease agreement for hardware that you will upgrade in two to three years can offer a seamless way to swap out obsolete equipment.

Leasing Types and Realities

Several types of lease agreements are available. However, they all fall into one of two categories that are referred to by different names depending on the financier. In general, you can recognize them as delineated in Table 5-1.

Table 5–1   Leasing Options

Options	Description	Advantages	Risks
"Fair Market Buy-Out"	Provides option to either purchase the hardware at the determined fair market value or allow you to give it back	Lower monthly payments Great for upgrading to new hardware	To keep the hardware at the end of the term will be very costly.
"Lease to Own"	Provides for ownership at the end of the term	Ensures ownership at term's end	You will have paid substantially more if hardware is obsolete at term's end.

Make no bones about it, leasing costs more than purchasing, no matter how the lease agreement is structured. The issue is the cost of money. The question is, "What is it worth to you (your company) to defer the cash layout of a purchase?"

The usability of the hardware at the end of the term determines which lease option is the best choice for you. The components of usability include the life span of the application and the obsolescence of the platform. Suppose that you are faced with a major upgrade of a legacy system to a newer version of that platform's architecture for capacity purposes. The application sitting on the legacy system is being re-built or strongly considered for rebuild on a client/server platform. This fact means that the application as it sits on the legacy system has a short projected life span. All estimates point to the fact that the rebuilt software will be completed within one year. This would be a good opportunity to choose the "Fair Market Buy-Out" option, as you plan for the phase-out or the end of life for the product. A good plan would call for a two-year term to account for a slip in the projection and also any parallel processing that would need to take place post-implementation. If something goes wrong with the projection two years from now, you will always have the option to buy the hardware at the lease term end.

▶ Cost of Implementation

No matter the size of the initiative, you will be faced with implementation resource challenges. Chances are that your operations staff is lean and mean, barely keeping up with business-as-usual challenges. Piling on one more, potentially huge initiative could cause an unacceptable deterioration in current performance and service levels.

You have two ways to develop the human resource needs for the initiative and the budget associated with them. If the project plan, referenced in Chapter Four, is complete, it will contain the staffing requirements based upon the time required to fulfill tasks and meet the milestones. If the plan is still under development, you can create a high-level estimate for budget purposes that you will reconcile to the detailed plan later. To create the high-level estimate, consider what human resources you have to work with in general and compare them to the data you collected when considering what components you are attempting to further automate and at what level.

To do so, take the technical planning and the decisions you've made in the build versus buy analysis above and engage your staff in the analysis. List each infrastructure component of your plan and discuss the projected time to manage the vendors, products, and/or in-house development efforts at hand. List each of the tasks required and project the amount of time to accomplish the tasks. Triple the time to account for natural inclination of techies to underestimate time requirements and to account for unforeseen needs. Then explore whether or not your personnel can realistically free up that kind of time to fully contribute to the implementation efforts.

Using Table 5–2 and working with your in-house staff to complete it will accomplish three important objectives. First, you will complete the first step to identify what your human resource requirements are. Second, you will quantify the in-house capability to fill the requirements and the gap of time that you don't have available. But most importantly, you will take a significant step in gaining buy-in from your staff when it comes to bringing in outside resources. This has been accomplished in two ways: first, they share ownership for the results now on paper, because they helped put it there, and two, they have firsthand awareness and understanding of why strangers are being brought in the building to "help."

Table 5–2   Resource Worksheet

Component/ Tasks	Skill Set—Function	Person Hours, by Time-Frame (in hours)	Resources Available	The Gap (%/Hours)
Performance Monitoring				
Project Management	Project Management	2000 x 60	10%	90% / 1800
Product Installation	System Administration	100 x 10	100%	0% / 0
Product Customization	S/W Development, Database Administration	2500 x 60	5%	95% / 2375
Testing	System Administration, Database Administration, Development Support	750 x 15	30%	70% / 225
Implementation	System Administration, Database Administration	500 x 10	50%	50% / 50
			Total Gap = 4450 Hours	

Be very sure to involve your techies in this exercise. Involving them in the thought and decision-making process will help ensure that you have their support if and when you do bring in outside resources to help manage and contribute to the implementation. Do not underestimate the importance of "buy-in" from your incumbent technical staff. Failure to achieve their support will expose your project to sabotage.

You now have an analysis of the personnel (time and positions) required to implement the automation initiative(s), and a documented assessment of the gap between existing and required resources. You will need to decide how to fill that gap—with new hires, contracted employees, or some combination thereof.

Ongoing Service

Ongoing service is going to be the toughest area for you to qualify for outsourcing. This comes down to the question, "Now that I'm liable to substantially change the way we manage this operation, do areas we administer now make sense to outsource to a third party?"

The answer lies in a very consistent set of criteria that you can use at any point to qualify whether or not you have an opportunity to outsource any service model. These criteria includes the following set of "True/False" statements:

- True/False: This is not our core competency.
- True/False: This is a potential vendor's core competency and, therefore, they should be able to do it better than we can.
- True/False: The potential vendor can provide the service more cheaply than we can provide it ourselves.

If the answer to any one of these is "False," forget it. Don't pursue an outsourcing initiative any further, even if the potential product or service is so titillating you can't imagine living without it. In certain situations in enterprise-sized outsourcing considerations, one of these criteria may be ignored for political reasons. But no consideration is imaginable, within the context of your data center automation initiative, to warrant outsourcing the ongoing service if it is your core competency, if the vendor can't do it better than you can, or if the vendor can't do it more cheaply. In all my experience, I have never worked with a company willing to spend more for quality when considering *outsourcing a data center operation,* unless political considerations were involved.

▶ Cost Benefit Analysis

Documenting the cost versus benefit of your initiative is one of the toughest things to do within an IT operational initiative. To quantify the "return" on the investment in hard cash is difficult. Unlike a marketing promotion, which requires an investment in the promotional activity and material that is more than offset by an increase in revenues, the automation initiative may be necessary simply to correct unacceptable performance.

Additionally, you are at a further disadvantage because you are analyzing an "automation" initiative that by definition suggests "savings." Your management is aware that you are preparing to increase automation. Unfortunately, they are likely to expect a dramatic reduction in head count and have probably figured out how they are going to spend the savings in other areas. This timeframe is where the planning you did in Chapter One to set realistic expectations for the level of automation you hope to achieve is really going to pay off.

Beyond staffing reductions, your cost benefit analysis shows the key benefits of automation and builds credibility. These are accomplished by employing the following strategies:

- Flat Growth
- Efficiency and Performance

Flat Growth

This is all about the infamous head-count issue.

If a reduction of head count has been your goal, now is the time to quantify it. You will need the list of components and automation objectives from Chapters One and Two. For purposes of discussion, the savings in a larger data center organization with a fairly complex automation initiative should be communicated as a percentage. For a smaller data center with a fairly low level of complexity, present the results in actual numbers. All in all, this point in time is where you're going to document the savings, in terms of staff reductions. Table 5–3 illustrates a likely scenario.

Table 5–3 shows what you can expect in reducing head count. Notice the Year 2 columns. On its face, a 0% reduction is not exciting. However, the automation initiatives allow the operations to grow without adding additional head count. Thus, the real benefit is not in reducing the existing head count. Instead, the benefit lies in slowing the rate of growth in data center staffing over time. This benefit assumes relatively moderate growth in initiatives that introduce new components as the second year commences.

Table 5–3 Staff Reduction Matrix

| Size of Operation | Complexity Level of Automation Initiative | Year One BAU | | Year One Automation | | Year 2 BAU | | Year 2 Automation | |
		%	Actual	%	Actual	%	Actual	%	Actual
5 (days) x 8 (hours) Staff of 5 2-6 Enterprise Platforms	Low to Medium	0%	0	0%	0	+5%	½	+0%	+0
5 x 24 Staff of 8 7-12 Enterprise Platforms	Medium	10%	1	5%	½	+10%	1½	+0%	+0
7 x 24 Staff of 12 13-20 Enterprise Platforms	Medium to High	20%	2	10%	1	+20%	2½	+0%	+0

Efficiency and Performance

One of the goals of your initiative is to augment the quality of processing and monitoring production operations. These increases in efficiency and performance generate benefits in much the same way you've demonstrated in the head-count objective through flat growth. Instead of numbers of reduced staff, the savings is expressed in hours saved due to more fully automating processes. These processes will reduce the amount of troubleshooting required as the combination of technical monitoring and enhanced administrative process components will create a more trouble-free environment.

To quantify time savings, list the technical and administrative process components you are working on (see Table 5–4). Also list specific areas of efficiencies you expect to gain in your initiative.

A word of caution: Any self-respecting executive will ask you to translate the efficiency gains into head-count reductions. Be prepared. Present the data center operations needs that have been given short shrift due to understaffing. If possible, include your executive's "hot buttons" in the list. For example, this project could be a pet project (make sure that it is timely) that has been repeatedly postponed. The point is to think through how your executive will respond to material. What questions will be asked? Prepare your responses accordingly.

Table 5–4 Efficiency Example

Component	General Enhancement Description	Efficiency Gains
Performance Monitoring / Capacity Planning (PM/CP)	Ability to configure system level, network, and database monitoring across multiple platforms from one administrative tool Automatic generation of system level, network, and database usage and trending reports	Hours per month saved in configuration maintenance Hours per month saved in troubleshooting Problems with capacity issues are automatically alerted, mitigating crisis

▶ The Financial Plan

Now that you have created output from the following exercises, it is time to wrap them together and create the Financial Plan, which contains the following components:

Introduction or Executive Summary—summarizes the key points of the budget and financial strategy:

- Capital Expenditures
- Operational Expenses
- Assumptions:
  - Hardware—Lease or Purchase
  - Software Purchase and/or Develop
  - Ongoing service
- Cost Benefit Analysis

The purpose of this exercise is to organize and prepare a document for both presentation and reference. The objective is to summarize your information in one place, using your company's accepted formats.

Communicating and Presenting The Plan

You have completed all the steps required to define and determine the cost-benefit of your automation initiatives. The work product from previous chapters is the input you need to create the presentation of the proposed initiative for approval. This is the last step prior to procurement and deployment:

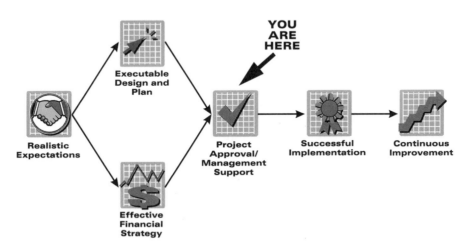

I took on a fairly lengthy engagement with a client whose needs for a production quality data center were increasing rapidly as the enterprise was in fast growth mode. The state I found it in was anything but "production." Subsequently, I found myself quickly pitching initiatives such as the ones described in this book. The interesting thing was that though the CIO would speak enthusiastically about building a world-class operation, the funding was apparently not there to back it. Or was it? Every time I approached the CIO with an initiative that I felt warranted serious consideration, I met tremendous resistance.

So I'd regroup and go back in and fight for what I needed. In the end, I never failed to get the proposals approved. But I did learn how to make life easier by giving him the information he needed in a form and sequence he required to make a decision. I learned that if I waited to spring a grandiose plan on him without prior, extensive priming, he'd hit the ceiling without regard for the merits of the proposal. I learned to plant seeds with him, succinctly articulate problem statements to him informally, and tell him I was going to go off and work on a solution, even though I already knew what it was. This approach engaged him, and I'd get feedback from him that would help me mitigate his objections later.

 As you read through this chapter, expect to find the answers to the following key questions:

- Who needs to know about this initiative and when?
- What does executive management need to know to approve the initiative?
- How do you build executive buy-in for the project in anticipation of a formal presentation?
- What other constituencies and audiences need to support the project?

▶ Building Support Among Key Constituencies

Communications are key to developing support for your automation initiative. And, you'll need that support not only to get your proposal approved, but also to ensure a successful deployment and adoption of the new technologies and processes. You must engage four constituencies very early in the process: IT staff, end users, management, and vendors. Let's review the opportunities that you have had thus far to engage, inform, and secure their support for the project (see Table 6–1).

Table 6–1   Engaging the Enterprise to Build Support

	Staff	End Users	Management	Vendors
Chapter 1: Setting Expectations	Validate complexities and set expectations		Review high level expectations Engage in the two-second reality check Validate that purpose has merit	
Chapter 2: Gathering and refining requirements (gap analysis)	Gather information Create problem/opportunity statements Validate requirements	Needs analysis (user requirements)	Gather information Validate problem/opportunity statements	
Chapter 3: Organization	Review structure and organization Validate job descriptions and functions		Validate structure and organization	
Chapter 4: Design and Planning	Manage design projects Participate in project teams Prepare or provide inputs to the plan	Participate in certain administrative process teams Validate dependencies and timelines of related or affected projects	Receive progress reports Validate dependencies	Respond to RFP Respond to questions; present proposal

Table 6–1 Engaging the Enterprise to Build Support *(continued)*

	Staff	End Users	Management	Vendors
Chapter 4: Financial Planning	Provide staffing information Assist with analysis		Receive briefing Provide guidance on lease vs. buy and other financial policies	Provide cost and staffing estimates
Chapter 5: Project Approval	Review presentation	Attend presentation as appropriate	Attend presentation Approve proposal	
Chapter 6: Deployment	Execute plan Risk analysis and contingency planning	Status reports	Status reports Conflict resolution	Development and execution

As Table 6–1 illustrates, you have had many opportunities to engage and inform key constituencies of the development of your automation initiative. For example, while completing the exercises in Chapter One, you should get input from your staff concerning the complexity level of the components and their expectations. Another good idea would be to inform your manager that you are beginning to research the feasibility of an automation project and to share your reasonable expectations concerning the purpose of the project and the projected automation enhancements. In this manner, you have informed management and engaged them in a reality check.

The activities of Chapter Two, the gap analysis, require involvement from your staff, end users, and management. Your staff should help you gather information, create problem/opportunity statements for each automation initiative, and validate requirements. They will also participate in meetings with end users to support the needs analysis. Finally, management should be kept involved, canvassed for input to the needs analysis, and be given the opportunity to validate the problem/opportunity statements. You have now built a second layer of commitment and buy-in. At this point, all your internal constituencies understand the purpose of the project, the opportunities associated with it, and the general scope of work.

In your review of the organization structure, you would need to involve your staff in any proposed changes to the enterprise services functions and responsibility assignments. In most organizations, your manager would need to approve any changes to the functional organization and/or position assignments. The composition and formal establishment of the project team is generally accompanied by a notification that would involve both staff and management.

As you enter the design phase, you have more opportunities to engage the enterprise and establish the basis for the ultimate approval of your initiative. Your staff will be thoroughly involved in the design of the technical architecture solution, the redesign of the administrative processes, and the evaluation of the technical tool sets to support the automated administrative processes. End users may participate in certain administrative process redesign activities such as those involved in production acceptance. In addition, you need input from the user community regarding dependencies and impacts on major business initiatives that should not be adversely affected by your project. Management should be periodically briefed, even if you include only updates on the project in your regular status reports. Also, you may have an opportunity to validate dependencies with management. Using these activities to engage in substantive communications about the project will build confidence in the initiative and your ability to lead it.

In addition to your staff, consider involving management and end users in some aspects of evaluation and selection of the technical tool sets. Be sure that vendor involvement is consistent to ensure fair play and objective recommendations.

The involvement of both staff and management in financial planning is outlined in Chapter Five. It includes getting the IT staff engaged in forecasting staffing requirements and the impacts of automation on future staffing needs. Seek out management advice regarding purchasing policies, lease vs. buy, insourcing vs. outsourcing, and other general directives. During these conversations, you'll be introducing high-level budget targets and investment strategies.

By the time you are ready to present this proposal, no surprises will occur. Staff, end users, and management are expecting a proposal and they have a very good idea about what will be in it. In fact, they have already had several opportunities to raise objections, identify risks, and clarify selection criteria. Expectations are realistic and clearly identified. The purpose of the project is well known. The timeline, overall cost, and staffing implications, both during the project and post-implementation, have been covered. Even the financing strategies have been discussed. All that remains is to gather your material and organize it into a succinct presentation that gets you to "yes."

▶ Gathering Information and Getting Organized

These are the reference materials that you and your staff have prepared that contain important information to include in your presentation:

- Project purpose statement: A one- or two-sentence statement that defines what you intend to accomplish (automation) and why (your success measure).
- High-level expectations: Define the level of automation that is realistic for each component in your environment.
- List of infrastructure components, with problem and opportunity statements, and automation requirements: Defines success on a component-by-component basis. Answers the questions "What problems are we going to solve?" and "What opportunities will we exploit?"
- Recommended system management software: A high-level description of the technical architecture solution, including insourcing vs. outsourcing.
- Revised administrative processes.
- Recommended tool sets to support automation of administrative processes that are the technical solution.
- High-level plan: Contains milestones, timeline, and resource requirements at a glance, on one page.
- Budget: Cost breakdown.
- Financial plan (financing strategy) and cost/benefit analysis.

With all this material, you have everything you need to prepare a compelling presentation and sell your initiative.

Use the simple outline in Table 6–2 to prepare your presentation. I have annotated each section with a brief description of what the section should contain, the approximate length, and the inputs to reference in preparing the slide and talking points. I would suggest that you prepare your presentation on overheads—what we refer to as "the deck"—with an executive summary in narrative form.

Table 6–2 Presentation Criteria

Outline Section	Content/Questions Answered	Reference Materials
Background One to three paragraphs in narrative form. Three to five bullets on a slide	**Why do we need more automation now?** Why is this project timely?	**High-level expectations** Problem and opportunity statements
Purpose Statement One or two sentences	**What is proposed?** What is the success measure(s)?	**Problem and opportunity statements**
Scope of work One slide for the components list One slide for the system management software One slide for the changes to the processes	Describes the bounds of the project—what is going to be automated and the design or solution for the automation Infrastructure components and level of automation associated with each one Technical architecture solution Revised processes and related tool sets	**Infrastructure component list and automation requirements** Recommended technical architecture solution Summary of change to administrative process
High-level plan Two slides	**Chart containing milestones, key dates, and staff requirements** Key Dependencies Project structure including team leads and team members	**Project Plan**
Budget and Cost/Benefit Analysis Three slides	**High-level capital and operating budget** Cost/benefit analysis Financing strategies (lease vs. buy)	**Financial Plan** Vendor proposals Internal proposals
Close One slide with a couple of bullets	**Request for authorization to proceed and:** Acquire or develop the solution sets Revise the processes Establish the deployment team	

After you have prepared your presentation, list all the questions that could arise, and make sure that you have reasonable answers to them. In some cases, you may want to include additional information in the presentation to address the obvious questions before anyone has a need or opportunity to ask them. This list of questions will also help you determine who should come with you to the presentation. You may have key staff members whose assistance will be valuable in responding to questions or even participating in the presentation.

Next, prepare your talking points. Finally, practice. You are already familiar with the content; now you need to get comfortable with the presentation format and the sequence of key messages.

Most presentations fail for one of three reasons: lack of preparation, surprising new material or issues, and failure to ask for authorization to proceed. Lack of preparation manifests itself in a number of ways: errors in the material, stumbling for words, inability to answer questions, poor organization or sequencing of information, and insufficient focus on the priorities. The second cause of failure is raising new issues or concerns. These should not come from you. Although you can't control what someone in the audience might think of and ask, you can control what you present. Again, nothing in this material should be new to your management if you have followed the methodology in this book. The third cause of failure would be neglecting to make a strong close. Remember, you are making this pitch to persuade management to sign off to procure the technology and begin deployment. Present your closing message with confidence and if they don't tell you to proceed, ask.

In closing, if you follow the guidance provided in this book, you'll have all the information required to prepare a compelling case. Plus, you will have buy-in before you give your presentation. Prepare carefully and sell with confidence.

Deployment and Continuous Improvement

You have completed the design and project planning. You have developed a financial strategy. And you have successfully obtained the approvals to begin the implementation and insertion of new technology. All your work to date is a setup for a successful implementation. Additionally, post-implementation, you will need to take steps to measure and evaluate performance, thereby ensuring continuous improvement. After all, are you ever finished? Do you reach that magic day when you put your feet up on the box and relax? I contend that the answer is no.

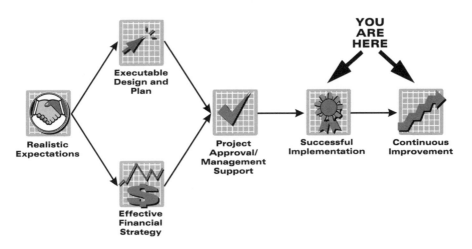

93

A few years ago, I led a group that accomplished a few significant tasks for a customer. The first was to move a computer room from one location to the next. The second was to design and deploy production (administrative) processes within their IS infrastructure operation. And the third was to establish a methodology and process by which the company could deploy its newly constructed client management system to its many remote sites nationwide. Of the three efforts, only the first was easily definable to management. The second and third were given attention by management only after much pain had been experienced. The pain around the deployment of the client management system came after many false starts attempting to deploy the software. They did not have a process to ready the sites, platforms, and the people responsible for managing them thereafter. Our focus on deployment processes resulted in an effective insertion of the technology as the project moved forward.

 As you read this chapter, you will find or develop the answers to these key questions:

- Does a significant difference exist between the technical deployment versus the administrative process automation? Should separate project champions manage them?
- What are the key pitfalls, and how can you avoid them?
- How do you manage for continuous improvement post-implementation?

In this chapter, we suggest that you organize the deployment activities by continuing the separation between the Technology Architecture and Administrative Processes. You'll recall that this separation was first introduced in Chapter Four. Note that risks and contingency planning described within the Technology Deployment section below also apply to the deployment of the technical tool sets that will automate the administrative processes.

▶ Technology Deployment

Have you ever heard the adage, "It is easier to build a house from scratch than remodel it"? Well, it is. Planning and scheduling for a remodeling project on your house always sounds great in theory. But the minute you open up a wall or floorboard and take a look at what's behind or beneath, you very likely have a whole set of issues and factors you didn't plan for and, subsequently, take you back to the drawing board. However, very often in these cases you are headed back to the drawing board with more than just what you found behind or beneath the façade. You now have the added factor that you have to patch up what you shouldn't have torn apart, anyway. This ends up costing you dearly in two very key areas, time and money.

Your technical automation initiative is a relatively significant remodeling effort. The same remodeling rules and "gotchas" apply. The best way to deal with this probability is to anticipate and plan for the unknown. But how?

To illustrate the point, refer back to the mock project plan in Figure 7–1. It has been enhanced with a sampling of the steps needed for deployment and it picks up where it ended in Chapter Four: Design and Planning.

For reference, the project plan above begins by listing only the summaries (denoted by a bold black line in the Gantt) and milestones (shown in italics and denoted by a diamond in the Gantt) from the Design and Planning section.

Assumptions and Risks

Naturally, the first task in technical architecture deployment comes from the established design, which contains the fundamental hardware and software requirements. Next, you will clarify assumptions, risks, and associated contingencies. This seemingly innocuous exercise is extremely important. Here's an example of how I got bit by not performing this task some time ago:

I led an effort to upgrade both the system and the storage subsystem of a relatively large platform for an undisputed mission-critical application. The priority focus of the project was the insertion of the storage subsystem, because it was delivering consolidated architectural benefits and administrative capabilities, which in turn delivered a more supe-

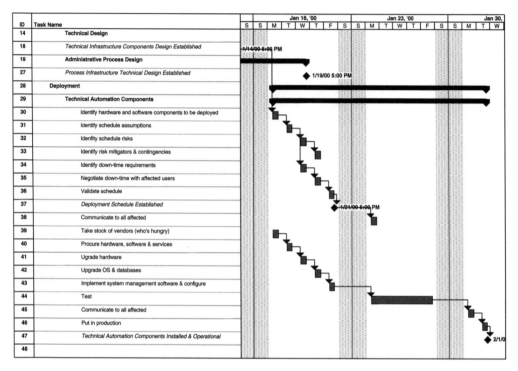

ID	Task Name							Jan 16, '00								Jan 23, '00								Jan 30,
		S	S	M	T	W	T	F	S	S	M	T	W	T	F	S	S	M	T	W
14	**Technical Design**																			
18	*Technical Infrastructure Components Design Established*		1/14/00 5:00 PM																	
19	**Administrative Process Design**																			
27	*Process Infrastructure Technical Design Established*								◆ 1/19/00 5:00 PM											
28	**Deployment**																			
29	**Technical Automation Components**																			
30	Identify hardware and software components to be deployed																			
31	Identify schedule assumptions																			
32	Idenfity schedule risks																			
33	Identify risk mitigators & contingencies																			
34	Identify down-time requirements																			
35	Negotiate down-time with affected users																			
36	Validate schedule																			
37	*Deployment Schedule Established*									◆ 1/21/00 5:00 PM										
38	Communicate to all affected																			
39	Take stock of vendors (who's hungry)																			
40	Procure hardware, software & services																			
41	Ugrade hardware																			
42	Upgrade OS & databases																			
43	Implement system management software & configure																			
44	Test																			
45	Communicate to all affected																			
46	Put in production																			
47	*Technical Automation Components Installed & Operational*																			◆ 2/1/0
48																				

Figure 7–1 Sample Automation Project Plan—Technical Automation Deployment

rior level of automation. One of the first tasks on the list was to replace a set of processors with more and a faster set of CPUs. Processors came from the same manufacturer, same box, same operating system, same everything. Simple, right? Unfortunately, we failed to assemble the team to brainstorm the risks and contingencies. So there we were, with everything lined up: supporting vendors, our own internal system and database administrators, and adequate downtime clearance—or so we thought. When the system vendor's field engineer arrived to witness the unpacking of the goods (hardware) and to facilitate the upgrade, she ran down her checklist and stopped us at the following validation point:

❑ Minimum OS version - X.x.x (specifics not revealed to protect the innocent)

What?! We were one release deficient and were now faced with upgrading the OS to meet the minimum configuration. Our upgrade window of time for the night shrank dramatically. "Abort or go for it?" We went for it. To make a long story short, the OS upgrade had its own significant problems, because it was done without planning assumptions, risk factoring, and related mitigators, and we aborted that night's efforts and went back to the drawing board. "Time – Money."

Now, you are probably thinking, "The oversight was too obvious." Any competent technical team would have planned for it. Well, that's my point exactly. Most often, the obvious stuff gets overlooked or someone assumes "I thought you had that one" and the sinking feeling that goes with it. These days, I develop risks and contingencies for every project, and I don't do it alone. I engage the staff so that we uncover the specific risks associated with the upgrade in the context of the particular data center environment that we are automating. I find that generic lists simply are not useful or complete. In fact, they may impart a false sense of security. The concept and methodology are important. Table 7–1 shows a sample checklist.

Table 7–1   Data Center Upgrade Assumptions/Risks Checklist

Assumptions	Responsible Party	Risks	Mitigators/ Contingencies
Hardware			
Arrives on time – Scheduled for <u>1/17/00</u>	Joe	It doesn't arrive on time	Schedule extra time in the project plan for late arrival
It works – Scheduled for 1/19/00 – 2/4/00	Bob	Dead on Arrival Powers up, but we have trouble configuring	Schedule extra time in the project plan for re-shipment Bring vendors on-site Identify technical alternative (vendor) and line up for emergency
Software			
Installs correctly and as advertised	Buford	Doesn't install correctly Have to call out for vendor assistance	Schedule extra time (in terms of "days" not "hours") for assistance Identify technical alternative (vendor) and line up for emergency

Table 7–1 Data Center Upgrade Assumptions/Risks Checklist

Assumptions	Responsible Party	Risks	Mitigators/ Contingencies
Configures as desired and as advertised	Buford	Does not configure as desired and advertised	Schedule extra time (in terms of "days" not "hours") for assistance
			Identify technical alternative (vendor) and line up for emergency
System			
Performs to specs, desires, and as advertised	Bob	Under-performs	Schedule extra time (in terms of "days" not "hours") for assistance
			Identify technical alternative (vendor) and line up for emergency

Notice the common sense aspect to this list. Not to mention the common problems. When you expand the list to include peripherals, subsystems, applications, and databases, you will have a comprehensive catalog of risks and contingencies that you can use to track formally. When the list is fully created, you can easily see how many seemingly simple issues can fall through the cracks.

Downtime

Downtime is a key issue to the scheduling aspects of the deployment. During the Gap Analysis, you identified, or at the very least validated, your system availability requirements. You will use that information now to determine what window(s) you have available to you to perform platform upgrades and system implementation.

Assess your scheduling input against the availability requirements of the mission-critical systems you will be working on. If you have the window(s) required to deploy your initiative without encroaching on your availability commitments, great! Move on to the following section on communication. If you do not have such a window, beg for it.

Now is the time to negotiate with the user community. The difficulty with this negotiation is that they have trouble recognizing any immediate benefit to them. Put on your deal-making hat. Be tactful. Promise priority response time from the help desk the next time they have a desktop need. Be resourceful. Be diplomatic. And if all else fails, escalate to executive management (e.g., the CIO).

Communication

Note that two tasks are captured in the mock project plan presented above that read "communicate to all affected." The first occurs right after you've established the schedule, and the second occurs during and after testing, prior to production. Though they are formally captured as tasks in the plan, I'm here to tell you that this should not be the only two times you communicate outside the group to those who care about what you are planning to do. I cannot stress enough the importance of proactive, effective communication. As pointed out in Chapter Six, it occurs everywhere in this methodology—when you are gathering requirements, presenting for approval, even in the design and planning.

In addition to providing useful information that people can act upon, you are also contributing to your own negotiating interests when negotiating breech of downtime to implement your initiative. Also, when problems occur, the users will have a basic understanding of your project to absorb the new information.

Testing

Notice that testing is the only task in the mock project plan that has more than a 1d (one-day) duration associated with it. I chose this to illustrate a point. In addition to being a responsible implementer by testing out your installation, you can make up unforeseen delays. A time cushion in the testing timetable can help you recover and deliver the solution on time. The time cushion is particularly important if you are running parallel systems or have time commitments to management or end users.

Test Criterion

In addition to giving yourself ample time to test and recover, of course you need to have the criterion by which you do the testing. In technical deployment, you will be dealing with two basic areas, hardware and software. In many cases, you will be dealing with them in the same exercise, since the two come hand-in-hand. An example would be the installation and testing of a sub-storage system that contains its own system management software.

Though your specific testing criterion requirements vary depending on the scope and complexity of your initiative, you should account for some basic criteria and apply them to your testing effort. They include:

- *Performance*—General performance objectives of the system you are testing, including hardware and software.

- *High Availability*—Redundancy abilities you expect your system to be able to handle.

- *Service Capabilities*—Automated third-party services being deployed.

- *Compatibility*—Connectivity or software and/or hardware integration issues.

- *Functionality*—Simply the functionality of the system desired.

- *Tool Management*—A specific subset of functionality.

- *Education/Training*—The ability to deploy the appropriate training to users of the system: could be in-house or third-party.

- *Price/Performance*—A validation that you are getting the optimal return for your investment.

To illustrate the details of these criteria, let's stick with the storage subsystem example and look at the sample test criteria listing in Document Sample 1.

Note that this is written to a third-party technology vendor providing this particular solution. You would not use all the criteria for an in-house developed solution. The good news is that you need only a subset of it. Eliminate 6 (Customer Education) and 7 (Price/Performance), and you have a healthy smattering of testing criteria.

Document Sample 1: Testing Criteria

IT Automation Initiative Testing Criteria—"Storage Sub-System"

1. Performance: XYZ software will measure processor utilization, disk utilization, and I/O response time. Data will also be collected for correlation with XYZ results. Two metrics will be evaluated: wall-clock time for large sequential application queries, and loads and disk busy for concurrent random operations. If the processor utilization is not a bottleneck, performance on the "Widget System" will be better than the current striped drives.

   Due to recent upgrades, to maintain performance parity, the sub-system must be capable of 2.5-fold more work. This will be determined by comparing the disk busy to processor busy ratio. To meet performance criteria, the subsystem under evaluation will need to decrease this ratio by a factor of 2.5. The "vendor" will have the opportunity to tune the "Widget System" to reach the acceptance criteria, including, but not limited to, reassigning data between volumes.

2. High Availability and Service: Failure insertion tests include failing a drive, wall power, cache, battery power, a power supply, a channel director, and a disk director. The "Widget System" feature, "ABC" will be tested during this procedure. The "Widget System" will perform to advertised specifications.

3. Compatibility: The "Widget System" will be addressed by the UNIX and the NT servers.

4. Software: "Widget System Manager" will work to advertised specifications.

5. Data Management: The "Widget System" will provide a central point of data management with flexibility and ease of use for all attached servers.

6. Customer Education: The designated test person at our company will understand the basic structure of the "Widget System" and be able to use the installed software. This will include ten hours training for the tester.

7. Price/Performance: Our company is evaluating an alternate storage sub-system during this period. If a more expensive sub-system is less than twice as much money but provides more than twice the performance, then it provides better value. If both sub-systems meet the basic performance criteria, then the sub-system with the better price/performance ratio is a better value.

▶ Administrative Process Deployment

As described in Chapter Four: Design and Planning, the design phase of the technical and administrative components share the methodology for evaluation and selection of technology. So also the deployment of the technology to support the administrative processes follows the same series of steps used to automate the technology architecture components. The narrative below describes the steps required to execute the redesign of the administrative process components, which is a complex and resource-dependent activity.

Refer once again to the mock project plan that contains summary tasks and milestones (see Figure 7–2)

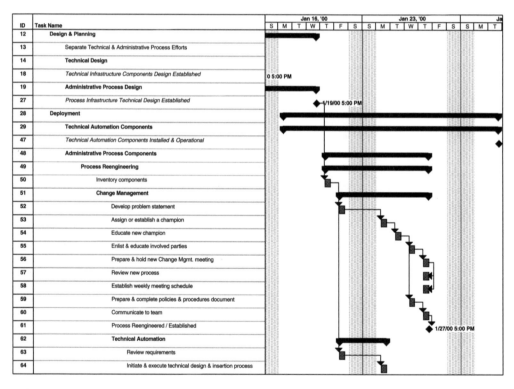

Figure 7–2 Sample Automation Project Plan—Administrative Process Deployment

Inventory

To begin, revisit the administrative processes that you are automating, and prioritize them for sequential deployment. Though in theory an organization could tackle multiple enhancements and changes to administrative process components, be sure to note that you will most likely not be successful doing so in parallel. These initiatives require significant resources and extensive training. Often, execution is painful because people have to change the way they perform certain functions. Changes or the insertion of new business processes is not trivial. I recommend staggering (overlapping project start dates) the deployment of the administrative process components, and at the very least—and if at all possible—linear execution (begin the next project start only after you have completed the last). You should have a leg up on "buy-in" if you involved the appropriate staff in the definition and redesign work described in Chapter Four.

That said, let's walk through the steps to deploy one of the administrative processes that all can relate to—Change Management—as an example of the activity required to enhance and automate the process.

Deployment Example—Change Management

The first thing to do is retrieve the problem statement you developed in Chapter Two and the process definition you revised in Chapter Four. The problem statement should contain the components you see below that are accompanied by two examples: the first for a process that needs enhancement and the second for one that does not exist and therefore needs to be created:

- The definition of current process:

    1st—*"The IS department of XYZ company currently employs an operational change management process. This process includes weekly meetings where operational members of the IS department meet to discuss activities in the data center environment."*

    or

    2nd—*"The IS department has no operational change management process."*

- Where the process is deficient:

  1st—*"Though the weekly meeting is informational, no identified, official chain of approval exists to effect change in the production environment. Post-mortem communication is informal (i.e., the hallway). In addition, little more than information communication exists to notify affected parties (i.e., users) of impending changes and the status of those just made. Emergency change control is just that, an emergency, with no controls in place."*

  or

  2nd—*"Changes to the production environment are informally, individually addressed, negotiated, communicated, and effected. No identified, official chain of approval exists. Post-mortem communication is informal (i.e., the hallway). In addition, informal communications are used to notify affected parties (i.e., users) of impending changes and the status of those just made. Emergency change control is just that, an emergency, with no controls in place."*

- Impact:

  1st—*"Lack of an appropriate request, approval, and communication process, exposes the production environment to ongoing problems, as ill-defined changes take hold. This compromises the integrity of the IS technical infrastructure."*

  or

  2nd—*"Lack of an appropriate request, approval, and communication process, exposes the production environment to ongoing problems, as ill-defined changes take hold. This compromises the integrity of the IS technical infrastructure."*

Notice that the impact statements are exactly the same.

The first job in assigning the work is to pick a process champion. You need to assign a person who will be responsible for implementing or enhancing this process. For more established shops, this might be the person who is already responsible for this activity and belongs to or represents the department's "production control" function and/or group. For a smaller group, this function may need to be established from scratch. In more mature IS organizations, I recommend a "Technical Process Architect" be established as a full time function (see Appendix B). The architect is responsible for all the administrative processes and supporting technology. This person can also double as a technical project manager for all infrastructure-related initiatives.

The responsibilities of the champion include:

- Implementing the new process.
- Chairing the weekly Change Management meeting.
- Developing and maintaining documentation of detailed processes.
- Facilitating all weekly communication.
- Facilitating the development and implementation of supporting automation technology(ies).

The next steps are education and training. Both the process champion and the individuals who participate in the process require training.

- Help Desk
- Networking
- Desktop Support
- Various Applications Development groups

- Server System Administration
- Data Base Administration
- Networking

First, work with the process champion or process owner, and provide education on the process and assistance with the development of the details and supporting materials needed to proceed with execution. Identify the key individuals that will represent the functional areas depicted above and then prepare for the new Change Management meeting. The individuals identified will make up the Change Management team. The purpose of this meeting is to present the new process, and invite discussion and input from the group concerning the content and how the team will work together (see Figure 7–3).

Figure 7–3   Change Management Process Flow

The champion will update and complete the Change Management Policies and Procedures document. Policy includes a definitive statement of "thou shall." Example:

> *"The Change Management team must approve all changes to the production environment. The IS VP must approve all emergency changes."*

The procedures describe how to execute the policy. This may be in a state of flux because the technical automation portion of this initiative will change the way the procedures are defined and executed. If so, define how it is done today and then manage the change in an iterative fashion. In either case, the procedures will contain the steps to take for requests, approval, and communication. The newly documented process, policy, and procedures should be communicated as soon as possible to the new Change Management team.

Summary

The key point in the deployment of your data center automation initiatives is to (a) split the technical architecture and administrative process implementation activities and manage them separately, and (b) sequence the integration of the redesigned administrative processes so that you deploy them one at a time.

▶ Continuous Improvement

Reporting

Continuous improvement begins with reporting that can be used to assess and fine-tune the performance of your newly automated operation. This section, similar to project management, is not a primer on the details of reporting within the enterprise. Additionally, you will note that reporting requirements are littered throughout the technical components you have defined, designed, and readied for deployment.

Make sure that you are capturing the right data at the right times for both technical process components and (administrative) management reporting. Table 7–2 contains the categories you need to capture in order to measure the quality of your environment:

Table 7–2   Performance Metrics

Metric	Requirement/Description
Systems Availability	• Availability within last 24-hour period (06:00 to 06:00 ET)
• System/Applications	• Sorted by Name of System and its Application(s) hosted
• Day/Hi	• Day = days system has been up w/out outage • Hi = system's best "up streak"
• Up Time	• Hours system has been up within the last 24-hour period
• Percent Up Time	• Percentage system has been up within the last 24-hour period
CPU Load Average	• 12 samples taken per day to make up daily and weekly averages

Percentage of CPU Utilized, Per Server
 	
  • Percent spent in I/O wait
  • Percent spend in user space
  • Percent idle
	• 6 - 12 samples taken per day, by filesystem, to make up daily and weekly averages

RAM Consumption • Paging and Swap Utilization	• 12 samples taken per day to make up daily and weekly averages

Disk Utilization, Per Server
 	
  • Kbytes Resident
  • Kbytes Used
  • Kbytes Available
  • Capacity (% of filesystem)
	• Reports by filesystem to make up daily and weekly averages

Application Activity
 	
  • Number Application Transactions
  • Response Time Average
  • Number Concurrent Users—High Water
  • Average Number Concurrent Users
	• Availability within last 24-hour period (06:00 to 06:00 ET)
	• *Total number of transactions during the period*
	• *Time it takes for user to complete transaction*
	• *Highest number of concurrent users at any given period of time*
	• *Average number of concurrent users within period*

Reporting and analyzing the output from Table 7–2 will tell you how to fine tune the technical operations to achieve improvements in performance and availability.

Administrative process components require continual measurement by the process owners and the team members who participate in their execution. The Enterprise (data center) Services director should use detailed data provided by these process owners to produce a "Management Metrics" report that compliments the Technical Metrics report above. Table 7–3 shows the categories and general metrics you will want to capture.

Table 7–3 Management Metrics

Metric	Requirement/Description
Request Activity:	●
● Number and Type of Requests	● Sorted by functional area
● Number of Requests	● Measured against number and type of requests for that time period
● Number of Requests Completed	● Measured against number and type of requests for that time period
● Number of Requests Pending	● Measured against number and type of requests for that time period
Problem Management:	●
● Total Number of Calls	● Trouble calls from users ● Sorted by functional area
● Number of Calls Closed	● Measured against number of calls for that time period ● Sorted by functional area
● Number of Open Calls	● Measured against number of calls for that time period ● Sorted by functional area
● Exception Reporting	● Those problems not resolved within commitment time and reason

This data can be captured in spreadsheets or databases, supported by graphics (pie charts, for example), and then integrated into publishing tools. Publishing tools can come in the form of documentation or even be integrated into "Intranets." Whatever method you choose, remember that a well designed, easy-to-understand report should make clear what is important and what requires a decision, change, or further monitoring. These reports are not a "data dump." They should be a well used and impressive addition to your operation. Your staff can also have some fun with the publication. Showcase your performance by providing quality information in a readable, accessible format.

Evolving

If you need to implement the methodologies and steps explained in this book, chances are that you are dealing with a dynamic and growing IT environment. So what do you do when you complete this initiative? Do what the coaches in the NFL do when they win on Sunday: smile, high-five, accept the acclaim, smoke a cigar, announce you're going to Disney Land, and then wake up on Monday and start planning for next Sunday.

"How do I do that?" you ask. "Haven't I just completed a major initiative to take my environment to the next level of automation? What's next?" Well, the place to start is the place you started. Go back to Chapter One, setting your expectations and completing your needs analysis. This information is still just as valuable to you as it was when planning your just-completed initiative.

The point is that the results of your "setting expectations" and "needs analysis" exercises probably did not justify a full-blown, highly complex automation of every technical and administrative process component. Probably you would like to have completed other projects but could not justify them at the time. Additionally, you and your staff probably learned a lot during the project. So go back to the original evaluation and analysis, update it, combine it with lessons learned, and repeat the process. Don't worry, though. The premise of the second and even third round is to improve incrementally and avoid wholesale changes. Regardless, the processes and methodologies are still valid and just as critical to your incremental success, just not as large and time-consuming as the first go-round.

Internal Service Levels

As an IT operations group, consider how the services you are providing the customer are meeting their needs. Historically, many exercises in creating and re-creating the dreaded Service Level Agreement (SLA) have been undertaken, with varying results. In my experience, much focus in the SLA effort is placed on the end-user-customer. I've found two fundamental challenges with this focus:

1. With the exception of the help desk and desktop support functions, we find that our primary customers are in our own house, within the IT organization.

   For example: Consider the applications developers as the primary customer to an IT operations group. They interface directly with the end user, making the end user secondary to operations.

2. If we haven't put our own house in order, how do we expect to service the outside/end customer well?

My answer is this: create an "Internal Service Level Agreement" with the rest of the IT organization. In doing so, you will find that you will achieve three benefits:

1. Services you can measure, manage, publish, and market.
2. Better interpersonal working relationships with your IT counterparts (i.e., development).
3. Much better situated to provide agreed-upon services that you can measure, manage, publish, and market to the outside end customers.

For a sample Internal Service Level Agreement, see Appendix C.

▶ In Closing

This book has given you the methodologies and steps necessary to take your current data center environment to the next step in automation and maturity. Let's review the methodology and the exercises one last time (see Table 7–4).

Table 7–4   Methodology and Exercise Review

Methodology	Exercises
Setting Realistic Expectations	Taking stock of Technical and Administrative Components
	Analyzing the complexity of your needs
	Identifying gaps and requirements
	Establishing realistic expectations
Organizational Assessment	Evaluating the organizational structure and functions versus industry standards and norms
Executable Design & Planning	Splitting Technical and Process efforts
	Identifying and selecting technical solutions
	Identifying new process objectives and definitions
Financial Planning	Identifying options
	Identifying benefits
Project Approval and Management Support	Marketing
	Presenting
Successful Implementation	Identifying assumptions, risks, mitigators, and contingencies
	Testing and execution
	Reengineering processes
	Inserting new technology
Continuous Improvement	Reporting and Reviews

Whatever your specific situation, the steps presented in this book are guidelines and references that take shape in the context of your unique data center, with the people, processes, and technologies of your organization.

Most Frequently Asked Questions

▶ People

Q1: *What increases in server-to-system-administration ratios would you expect to see once you've automated your mission critical production environment?*

A1: Admittedly, this question is the most difficult to answer. Ratios will depend greatly on the scope of your initiative. As you read in Chapter One, the first step in your effort will be to evaluate the core data center components you will consider for automation. The next step is to evaluate and choose the level of automation you will undertake for each component. The results of these decisions will provide a basis for determining the ratio. The trick is to use the data these exercises produce to realistically back into the ratio you are trying to achieve. See Chapter Five for more details concerning defining and setting staff reduction expectations.

Q2: *Will we have morale issues to deal with as we're attempting to implement a lights-out environment?*

A2: Morale issues are a large concern of this initiative. The key is to involve your technical staff in the planning and even presentation of the project. Early and close involvement by your staff will address several personnel issues presented by this initiative, including buy-in, ownership, and the ability and willingness to execute. Additionally, the issues of how the initiative will affect their jobs should be discussed explicitly and in as much detail as possible during the planning stages.

Most IT technical professionals are so overwhelmed with work that any reduction in workload is a welcome proposition. And remember, techies love tech. Reinforce the positive aspects of the opportunity to work on leading-edge technology, project management, and implementation this initiative will provide. Change is always a tough aspect of the workplace to manage. Don't shy away from it. Take it head on. Staff will both appreciate it and benefit from it.

Q3: *I still have a large mainframe staff—should I get them involved with designing a new data center?*

A3: This book does not focus on the integration of legacy operations into distributed computing. However, it very strongly implies and recommends that an automation initiative presents the opportunity to do just that. With minor technical adjustments, data center processes are a ubiquitous proposition for all data centers, no matter what the central technology platforms. You have network requirements, database requirements, stabilization requirements, scheduling requirements, etc. Remember that the network is the data center. You must consider all technical platforms in the initiative, including the network itself. That said, mainframe personnel should be included right alongside other technical staff.

Additionally, mainframe personnel provide you with an even more exciting upside. Chances are that they are a little intimidated by distributed computing, but more than happy to get a chance to grow with it. Addressing the impact on their jobs directly with them creates an interesting career path, mentoring, and career development opportunities.

Q4: *I'm in charge of the infrastructure in my company. The CIO came from the business unit—he has no clue as to what benefits can be achieved. Most of his budget goes toward applications development efforts. How do I sell the benefits that could be gained by having a lights-out data center?*

A4: Marketing, marketing, marketing. This is achieved through a simple process of early and sustained communication, solicitation of input to not only the CIO, but also your counterparts who will also benefit from the initiative. You will need both buy-in and resources from groups, such as applications development to succeed in the initiative. This kind of communication creates synergy and ownership across the whole IT organization, bridging the gap between apps and ops. See Chapter Six for more details on selling the initiative. Also, Chapters One and Two contain tips on getting CIO buy-in and involvement early—these tips are particularly critical in the case described in Question Four.

Q5: *Which part of the organization is responsible for architecture and design of the lights-out plan? How many people and which parts of my staff will need to be involved with the overall implementation?*

A5: Operations takes the lead (a.k.a. Enterprise Services, Infrastructure, etc.). In a networked environment, you will need representation from all the functional groups within the IT operations organization, including system administration, networking, database administration, production control, etc. Also, as technology comes into play, representation from the applications side of IT will be needed. See Chapter Three, which has a section on putting together the "light-out" project team.

Q6: *Do special training requirements exist for the folks implementing this new lights-out environment?*

A6: Although no such thing as "automation" training exists, you can bet that training is an important aspect of deployment in two areas. First, employees who are using new technologies will need to become proficient in the operation and integration of the new hardware, software, and systems. Second, the administrative process changes will require training to ensure that they are correctly defined and consistently applied. See Chapter Four for more details.

If you follow this approach and methodology outlined in this book, the employees that require training will be involved in the project from needs analysis through deployment. No one will be surprised that they need to learn something new. In fact, they will participate in the decisions and at least some of the training will occur during the analysis, design, and planning stages.

Q7: *Will a reduction in staff occur once you implement a lights-out environment?*

A7: Depends on you. However, if you want my recommendation, consider a dual objective to slow the rate of staff growth and optimize the resources you have, instead of cutting positions. See Q1 earlier and Chapter Five.

Q8: *Will I need to restructure my organization at any time throughout this endeavor?*

A8: This initiative provides an ideal time to look at reorganization issues. In fact, it may be critical to the success of the project. If your organization does not contain the core functions described in Chapter Three (further identified in job descriptions in Appendix B), you'll have trouble implementing an automation project. The automation initiative will create changes in processes, i.e., the way people work and what they work on. If your organizational structure is both sound and complete going in, the deployment and associated changes will be much easier to complete. This issue is extremely important and is covered in some detail in Chapter Three.

Q9: *Will the customers see a better level of service? Will overall customer satisfaction improve?*

A9: They had better. In Chapters One and Two, you will scope the project on the basis of problems to be solved or opportunities to exploit in each of 15 technical and administrative process areas. No automation will be undertaken unless driven by definable improvements in performance and/or nagging problems solved. Thus, from the very beginning of this project, you will be defining the outcomes in terms of improved performance that should make all your customers, both inside and outside of IT, very happy.

Q10: *Who or which group in the organization would own the overall project plan?*

A10: The data center manager or director should own the plan. If you have played your cards right, the CIO will be your project champion—see tips in Chapters One, Two, and Three.

▶ Processes

Q1: *I don't have the time or the resources to implement all the processes you recommend. Which ones are the most critical?*

A1: This is another one of those "it depends" answers. It depends on the strengths and weaknesses of your data center environment. However, I can offer some clues. In my experience, certain components seem to be consistently problematic or critical for enhancement. Among the technical architecture components, these include Performance Monitoring/Capacity Planning and the relationship between Scheduling and Event Monitoring. Among the process architecture components, Production Acceptance, Problem Management, and Change Management consistently require extensive enhancement and automation.

But don't adopt my generic assessment. Apply the exercises in Chapters One and Two, and you'll come up with your own list of high-priority, high-return process improvement/change opportunities.

Q2: *Which metrics should I be tracking before and after I design a lights-out data center to assure that I'm seeing benefits?*

A2: The high-level metrics I recommend include (see Chapter Seven for supporting criteria details):

- System Availability, including day/hi, uptime, and percent available.
- Network Availability, including summarized utilization and percent available per segment and overall—and conversely, downtime per segment and overall.
- Problem Management, including number of calls and open tickets, turnaround time per category (to match your objectives), and exceptions.

▶ Technology

Q1: *How do you deal with a heterogeneous data center for process ownership and tool selection?*

A1: In a networked data center, process ownership should be centralized even if technical support is distributed across platforms. Processes such as Change Management need to have a central champion to ensure the success of the process. Heterogeneous requirements are considered during the analysis process. The consideration for automating multiple platforms will heavily affect time, scope, and budget around people and technology, as the complexity increases exponentially with each platform considered. See Chapter Four.

▶ General

Q1: *What are the costs associated with automating my Data Center?*

A1: The answer depends on the scope of your initiative. If you follow the methodology in this book, you will define what and how much to automate based upon realistic expectations, opportunities for performance improvement, and nagging problems you need to solve. Although the specific expenditures will vary by project, you will undoubtedly have some combination of capital expenditures and operational expenses. These will be affected by your decisions regarding lease vs. buy, insourcing and outsourcing, and a host of other factors detailed in both the design (Chapter Four) and the financial plan (Chapter Five).

In addition, Chapter Five gives you the tips and tools to develop a financial case, but don't forget to ask, "What is it going to cost us if we don't?"

Q2: *When you design a lights-out data center, how would you incorporate all your remote server rooms—or should they be incorporated at all into your overall plan?*

A2: The network is the data center. Technical platforms and geographical locations should all be managed under one data center process scheme.

Q3: *The term "lights-out" has been around for two decades now— why hasn't it become reality as of yet?*

A3: Frankly, "lights-out" is a misnomer. In its purest definition, it is not reasonably obtainable. No Enterprise Services Director really "turns off the lights" and goes home to let the data center run itself.

Perhaps more importantly, increased automation poses an interesting problem. The paradox is this: the more bells and whistles you add to the environment, the more moving parts you have to manage. The fewer moving parts, the better. The key is to set yourself and your organization up for success. Moderate your enthusiasm for automation by developing realistic, obtainable goals. Then plan and execute an automation project that delivers on those goals. The exercises presented in Chapter One (setting realistic expectations) are the first and most important steps you must take.

Q4: *Wouldn't outsourcing the entire data center be cheaper than all this work of designing and implementing a lights-out environment?*

A4: It might. However, you can't make the decision without setting expectations, defining requirements, and performing the gap analysis. In fact, in design (Chapter Four), you'll consider the pros and cons of outsourcing, and I recommend that you issue RFPs to both internal and external sources. Let your staff compete with the vendors but do so against a consistent set of requirements and selection criteria. If total outsourcing is the answer, it will become apparent as you apply the methodology.

Q5: *How much time do I need to implement a lights-out environment? Can I do it in increments?*

A5: Time depends on scope. The good news is that the project can be scheduled and deployed incrementally. In Chapter Four, you'll separate the technical and administrative process components for design and planning purposes; you'll do the same in Chapter Seven, which covers deployment. In this book, we suggest that you work on the technical architecture and process architecture in parallel, but sequencing works, too. Specifically, you can change the process architecture first, and deploy new technical architecture tools or systems over time.

Q6: *What are the top priorities to focus on when implementing a lights-out environment?*

A6: People first, administrative processes second. The people issues include staff involvement, executive management communication, coordination with other IT functions (i.e., applications development), and organizational structure. People issues are dealt with over and over again in every chapter of this book, because no step in the methodology can be successfully completed without the proper engagement of personnel. See particularly Chapters Three and Six.

The second priority is the definition and deployment of new or changed administrative processes. As stressed in Chapter Four, the single, most frequent source of failed automation initiatives is poorly defined, inadequately addressed administrative processes.

B

Enterprise (Data Center) Services

▶ Sample Organization and Management Job Descriptions

Figure B–1 shows a sample personnel organizational chart that can be mapped back to the functional chart used for reference in Chapter 3.

As the leaders of the IT Enterprise (data center) Services group, we have provided detailed job descriptions and missions for senior management:

- Enterprise (Data Center) Services Director
- Computer Operations Manager
- Network (WAN) Infrastructure Manager
- LAN (Desktop) Administration Manager
- End User Services Manager

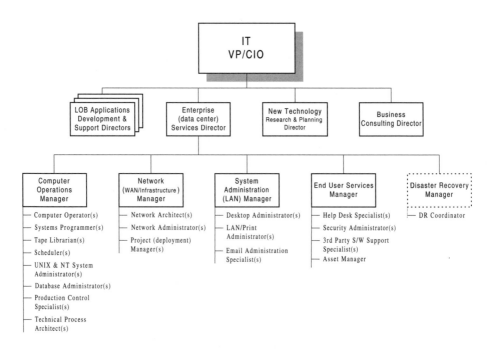

Figure B–1   Sample Personnel IT Organization Chart

Enterprise (Data Center) Services Director

Purpose

Builds, manages, and maintains the architecture and operations to deliver high-availability, enterprise-wide computing and production services, and to support new and changing applications.

Key Responsibility Areas

Technical Performance

- Manages the systems, databases, network, and operational components of the enterprise to meet performance requirements for availability and responsiveness.
- Maintains cost-effective end-user services and assets to support end-user computing requirements.

- Creates a consolidated and comprehensive disaster recovery strategy and executable plan within time and cost constraints.

Management and Communications

- Provides technical direction to staff, peers, and subordinate management; ensures that technical and process architectures are designed and operate to support business requirements.
- Establishes effective internal and external relationships.
- Develops and executes staffing plans. Supports, reviews, and approves personnel moves, ads, changes, and performance issues for direct reports.
- Approves project initiatives by authorizing scope, approving resources, managing risks, and approving changes in scope, schedule, and budget.

Planning and Forecasting

- Develops and maintains annual plans and budgets; prepares re-forecasts and other budget management tools and reports as required.

Performance Measures and Expectations

Establishes and meets/exceeds service level commitments as defined with IT management, consistent with user-community requirements.

Operates reliable, available, and responsive mission-critical systems, per industry standards in similar environments.

Incorporates user satisfaction in regularly scheduled reporting.

Education and Experience

MS or MA in computer science, business, other related field, or equivalent. Ten years of data communications systems management, including at least five years middle (IT) management experience, or the equivalent in a combination of education and experience.

Knowledge, Skills, and Abilities

Extensive and demonstrable proficiency in automated IT production infrastructure support processes, data communications, data center platform architecture, and project management.

Experience in managing and leading managers, individuals, and teams. Ability to plan for the hiring, recruiting, and motivation of a professional work force.

Ability to work within and lead groups so that the group is successful and productive.

Ability to develop and present a business case to support the infusion of new technologies and automation to improve infrastructure performance.

Excellence in preparing and delivering written and oral communications to achieve stated objectives.

Ability to identify and sequence actions to achieve goals while mitigating possible risks.

Ability to estimate expenses and calculate return on investment and total cost of ownership.

Computer Operations Manager

Purpose

Manages the architecture and computer operations of the data center to deliver high-availability, mission-critical production services.

Key Responsibility Areas

Technical Performance

- Develops, manages, and automates operations to improve performance, expedite problem resolution, and maintain assets.
- Creates and implements production control processes to perform production acceptance, change management, and scheduling.

- Establishes, maintains/enhances platform architecture.
- Administers, develops, and oversees the database to ensure data integrity and data quality.
- Implements and oversees the system programming, performance, and tuning operations and processes.

Management and Communications

- Creates productive relationships with vendors and consultants to resolve operational issues and execute approved initiatives.
- Coordinates and manages cross-functional projects with peers and end users. Develops and maintains reliable internal relationships.
- Manages the recruitment, selection, development, and performance of assigned staff to sustain or improve data center performance.
- Manages projects to deliver milestones on time and within approved budgets.
- Prepares and presents performance reporting.

Budgeting and Planning

- Creates and validates disaster recovery plans and resource requirements, including training and regularly scheduled practice sessions.
- Develops the annual data center budget, operations, and staffing plan.

Performance Measures and Expectations

Maintains or enhances the stability of the current data center infrastructure as measured and communicated in scheduled reporting.

Meets service level commitments for the reliability, availability, and responsiveness of mission-critical systems.

Education and Experience

BS or BA in computer science, business, or other related field, and five years experience as a Data Center and/or Operations Manager; or a combination of education and experience providing equivalent knowledge.

Knowledge, Skills, and Abilities

Experience and proficiency in the organization and administration of data center operations and processes and technical implementation.

Ability to plan, hire, manage, evaluate, and motivate staff.

Skillful communicator; able to present complex technical information to non-technical and/or technical audiences with equal success in written or oral communications.

Ability to identify and sequence activities and dependencies to achieve objectives while considering and mitigating possible risks.

Skill in organizing, segmenting, and delegating work to meet priority responsibilities and sustain performance.

Ability to analyze problems and develop and execute solutions under time and resource constraints. Ability to identify causes and implement operational changes to prevent reoccurrence.

Ability to define, scope, and manage projects to completion, reporting on progress as necessary and appropriate.

Network (WAN) Infrastructure Manager

Purpose

Plans, develops, and manages the WAN and overall network infrastructure to deliver the required connectivity, availability, and performance.

Key Responsibility Areas

Technical Performance

- Manages the architecture and infrastructure to meet performance requirements for availability and responsiveness.

- Maintains cost-effective support services and assets to maintain and enhance performance; manages upgrades and changes.
- Creates a coordinated and comprehensive disaster recovery strategy and executable plan within time and cost constraints.
- Provides overall architecture and direction to LAN Administration groups and personnel.

Management and Communications

- Provides technical direction to staff and peers; ensures that technical and process architectures are designed and operate to support business requirements.
- Establishes effective vendor relationships; evaluates new product and service offerings.
- Develops and executes staffing plans. Supports, reviews, and approves personnel moves, ads, changes, and performance issues for direct reports.
- Approves project initiatives by authorizing scope, approving resources, managing risks, and approving changes in scope, schedule, and budget.

Planning and Forecasting

- Develops and maintains annual plans and budgets; prepares re-forecasts and other budget management tools and reports as required.
- Creates outsourcing plans and budgets.

Performance Measures and Expectations

Operates a reliable, available, and responsive WAN, per industry standards in similar environments.

Incorporates vendor reporting with internal documentation.

Education and Experience

MS or MA in computer science, business, other related field, or equivalent. Five to ten years of data communications systems management, including at least two to four years (IT) management experience, or the equivalent in a combination of education and experience.

Knowledge, Skills, and Abilities

Extensive and demonstrable proficiency in full data communications and telecommunications architecture, design, planning, implementation, and support. Good knowledge of key industry leaders.

Experience in managing and leading individuals and teams. Ability to plan for the hiring, recruiting, and motivation of a professional work force.

Ability to work within and lead groups so that the group is successful and productive.

Ability to develop and present a business case to support the infusion of new technologies and automation to improve infrastructure performance.

Excellence in preparing and delivering written and oral communications to achieve stated objectives.

Ability to identify and sequence actions to achieve goals while mitigating possible risks.

Ability to estimate expenses and calculate return on investment and total cost of ownership.

LAN (Desktop) Administration Manager

Purpose

Builds, manages, and maintains the local area network, including desktop and print services to ensure the required end-user functionality and productivity.

Key Responsibility Areas

Technical Performance

- Manages the architecture and standards to meet system requirements for existing and impending desktop functionality.

- Manages operational needs of the local area network connectivity and infrastructure, including desktop print services.
- Maintains cost-effective support services and assets to maintain and enhance performance; manages upgrades and changes.
- Creates a coordinated and comprehensive disaster recovery strategy and executable plan within time and cost constraints.
- Provides overall architecture and direction to LAN Administration groups and personnel.

Management and Communications

- Provides technical direction to staff and peers; ensures that technical and process architectures are designed and operate to support business requirements.
- Establishes effective internal and external relationships.
- Develops and executes staffing plans. Supports, reviews, and approves personnel moves, ads, changes, and performance issues for direct reports.
- Approves project initiatives by authorizing scope, approving resources, managing risks, and approving changes in scope, schedule and budget.

Planning and Forecasting

- Develops and maintains annual plans and budgets; prepares reforecasts and other budget management tools and reports as required.

Performance Measures and Expectations

Establishes and meets/exceeds service level commitments as defined with IT management, consistent with user community requirements.

Incorporates user satisfaction in regularly scheduled reporting.

Meets problem management performance metrics, interacting and cooperating with End User Services' Help Desk operations.

Education and Experience

MS or MA in computer science, business, other related field, or equivalent. Five to seven years of data communications systems management, including at least two to four years (IT) management experience, or the equivalent in a combination of education and experience.

Knowledge, Skills, and Abilities

Extensive and demonstrable proficiency in desktop architecture, testing, deployment, and support.

Experience in managing and leading individuals and teams. Ability to plan for the hiring, recruiting, and motivation of a professional work force.

Ability to work within and lead groups so that the group is successful and productive.

Ability to develop and present a business case to support the infusion of new technologies and automation to improve infrastructure performance.

Excellence in preparing and delivering written and oral communications to achieve stated objectives.

Ability to identify and sequence actions to achieve goals while mitigating possible risks.

Ability to estimate expenses and calculate return on investment and total cost of ownership.

End User Services Manager

Purpose

Manages end-user computing support services, including problem management, third-party software support, security administration, and software/hardware asset management to consistently deliver cost-effective performance and productivity.

Key Responsibility Areas

Technical Services

- Manages the problem management process and system.
- Evaluates new third-party products and manages upgrades and new product introductions, as well as vendor interface and management.
- Performs asset management, including the procurement process, incoming product, transfer of assets, inventory, and the "end-of-life" process.
- Manages adds, changes, and deletions of users to systems, networks, applications, and databases.

Management and Communications

- Creates productive relationships with vendors and consultants to resolve operational issues and execute approved initiatives.
- Coordinates and manages cross-functional projects with peers and end users. Develops and maintains reliable internal relationships.
- Manages the recruitment, selection, development, and performance of assigned staff to sustain or improve data center performance.
- Manages projects to deliver milestones on time and within approved budgets.
- Prepares and presents performance reporting.

Budgeting and Planning

- Evaluates and justifies new product introductions and upgrades.
- Researches and creates annual plans and budgets.

Performance Measures and Expectations

Meets service level commitments for the turnaround of problems in the enterprise, consistently reporting on numbers, status, and exceptions.

Provides an efficient procurement and end-of-life process and up-to-date inventory data.

Manages and reports on user and customer satisfaction.

Education and Experience

Certification and/or degree from a technical trade school or equivalent experience. BS or BA degree in computer science, business administration, or related field recommended. Three to five years in end-user computing and two years of management experience, or the equivalent in education and experience.

Knowledge, Skills, and Abilities

Experience and proficiency in help desk management and customer service.

Knowledge of security administration, asset management, contract management and project management.

Ability to plan, hire, manage, evaluate, and motivate staff.

Skillful communicator; able to present complex technical information to non-technical and/or technical audiences with equal success in written or oral communications.

Ability to identify and sequence activities and dependencies to achieve objectives while considering and mitigating possible risks.

Skill in organizing, segmenting, and delegating work to meet priority responsibilities and sustain performance.

Ability to analyze problems and develop and execute solutions under time and resource constraints. Ability to identify causes and implement operational changes to prevent reoccurrence.

Ability to define, scope, and manage projects to completion, reporting on progress as necessary and appropriate.

Individual Contributor Roles/Purposes

Now that we've taken a look at the roles, purpose, and mission of the leaders in the Enterprise (data center) Services group, I offer the following purpose statements to provide a definition for the individual contributors that support them:

Computer Operator—Oversees established technical processes for enterprise-sized servers and peripherals to provide watchdog monitor and response service to mission-critical systems.

Systems Programmer—Evaluates, tests, and deploys system management tools to all server platforms to provide insertion and optimization of technology and process that make up computer operations.

Tape Librarian—Organizes, stores, and manages the movement of tape storage systems, devices, media, and processes to ensure that critical enterprise data is stored and recoverable for operations and disasters.

Scheduler—Oversees job scheduling and scheduling tools for production system routine events and processes to provide a technical scheduling infrastructure capable of handling new and changing requirements.

UNIX & NT System Administrators—Manages server implementation and ongoing administration to ensure system level—operating system, scripting, hardware, sub-systems, and peripheral—operational enhancement and stability.

Database Administrator—Manages the ongoing operational needs of the production database, including schedules, sizing, performance, enhancement, revisions, etc., to ensure required availability and performance.

Production Control Specialist—Manages the process architecture components of the data center (i.e., Production Control and Change Management) to ensure the stability and availability of the production environment as a whole.

Technical Process Architect—Working as a technical project manager with both the production control specialist and representatives of technical process architecture, manages the insertion and enhancement of production quality processes to ensure the enterprise adjusts to and/or adds to infrastructure to meet changing requirements and remain stable and available.

Network Architect—Evaluates, architects, designs, and inserts new network technologies into the enterprise as a whole to meet new and changing requirements.

Network Administrator—Manages the technical and process components that make up the wide area network—such as hardware, software, service vendors, etc.—interacting with local area network personnel to ensure ongoing stability and availability.

Network Project (deployment) Manager—Manages new technical network initiatives from design and into production operations to provide the project management needed to ensure smooth deployment.

Desktop Administrator—Builds, tests, deploys, and provides ongoing management of the desktop for the enterprise to ensure user functionality.

LAN/Print Administrator—Deploys and manages the hardware and software required to provide local area network services—including print—to IT and user communities.

Email Specialist—Provides support of third-party email systems (i.e., Lotus Notes) that require specific subject matter expertise (this position is required if the system is a specialized email application).

Help Desk Specialist—Provides interface to the user community and facilitates support as a coordinator to the technical support teams to identify, track, and solve IT-related problems.

Security Administrator—Manages (adds, changes, deletes) access administration to the network and production applications and data for IT and the user community.

Third-Party S/W Support Specialist—Manages the vendors that provide third-party software to provide published information for the IT community, contract administration and vendor relations.

Asset Manager—Tracks, stores, and manages the technical assets of the company to provide central administration, a data repository, and end-of-life services.

Disaster Recovery Coordinator—Develops, plans, and coordinates all disaster recovery exercises, soliciting involvement from other organizations to establish an ongoing disaster recovery exercise schedule.

Sample IT Operations Internal Service Level Agreement

SAMPLE

**IT Operations
Internal Service Level
Agreement**

Between IT Operations

and

The Information Technology Organization

Effective *(Date)*

Version 1.0

135

Overview

This Internal Service Level Agreement is an agreement between IT operations and the IT organization to support all key functional areas within IT: the different applications and product development, business systems, and technical architecture. Although these functional areas are tightly coupled, their IT service requirements differ in time frame and scope.

The objective of the Internal Service Level Agreement is to arrive at a mutually satisfactory consensus for services provided by IT operations to the IT organization as a whole. This will be accomplished by identifying and documenting the guidelines and responsibilities of each party. The goal is to ensure complete compliance, in order to achieve maximum quality, and efficiency for the IT organization by IT operations. In addition, this agreement will establish quantifiable and measurable requirements for acceptable service, and provide a formal system by which service can be measured and tracked.

This Internal Service Level Agreement covers the relationship between the parties to the agreement as it pertains to escalation procedures, incident ownership, update and closure processes, and internal customers interaction.

This Internal Service Level Agreement will be reviewed on a semi-annual basis, unless specific reasons necessitate additional reviews. The review will be conducted by the authorizing parties identified in the Approval section of this agreement. This agreement shall become effective on (effective date), and will remain in effect for a term until such time as the agreement has been renewed or a new agreement comes into effect.

Information Technology Organization

Internal Service Level Agreement

Online/Access Availability Requirements

Application Development
7x24 Minus Scheduled Downtime
The above availability times are covered by this SLA.

Product Development
7x24 Minus Scheduled Downtime
The above availability times are covered by this SLA.

Business Systems
Eastern Standard Time Availability Window
Monday - Friday   5 AM - 8 PM
Saturday   7 AM - 8 PM
Sunday   9 AM - 7 PM
The above availability times are covered by this SLA.

Technical Architecture
See SLA Billing
The above availability times are covered by this SLA.

Note: Changes to applications, databases, and subsystem schedules that affect the availability window identified in this SLA need to be approved by the Change Review Board.

Normal weekly maintenance for Web-based and client/server operations is scheduled for 1:00 AM to 9:00 AM CST every Sunday. Access is generally not available during this period. Weekday Business Systems general availability is 5X24 minus scheduled outage times of 8:00-

8:30PM and 1:00-2:00AM CST. Every effort is made to minimize the need for any additional outages.

Measurements

Application and Product Development

A service baseline of 97.5% availability has been established. This number is derived from the 1998 year-to-date availability average. Effectiveness will be measured against this baseline with a joint understanding that 100% availability is the objective for the times specified in this SLA. IT operations produces charts to measure monthly availability for end-to-end order processing. Measurement data on the effectiveness of the IT operations process can be accessed through the Web on http://www.intranet.com/it/operations/support. This information is based on the data available to IT operations. Our customers need to be able to gather information regarding access, performance, and unplanned outages that need to be addressed in the SLA review process.

Business Systems

A service baseline of 99.5% availability has been established. Effectiveness will be measured against this baseline with a joint understanding that 100% availability is the objective for the times specified in this SLA. IT operations produces charts to measure monthly availability for end-to-end order processing. Measurement information on the effectiveness of the IT operations process data can be accessed through the WEB on http://www.intranet.com/it/operations/support. This information is based on the data available to IT operations. Locations need to gather information regarding access, performance, and unplanned outages that need to be addressed in the SLA review process.

Customer Service Contract

Client/Web Services

Services	Description	Specifications
Processors and operating systems	Server systems will include both central and remotely managed systems that provide for the development and ongoing support within the IT organization. Key Components defined include: UNIX centralized and remote UNIX centralized NT centralized	Client servers will be available Monday - Friday 5 AM - 8 PM Saturday 7 AM - 5 PM Sunday 9 AM - 7 PM
Data bases management systems	Sybase SQL, Oracle	
Servers D/B	Web Hosting ABC and associated D/B's	
Applications	ABC XYZ	

Midrange
Services

Services	Description	Specifications
Processor & operating systems.	Midrange systems will include both central and distributed systems that provide for the development and ongoing support within the IT organization.	Centrally managed servers for will be available 7X24 minus scheduled backups.
Database management systems	Oracle MPE/Image	
Mid-range databases		
UNIX applications	PMCS MDCS, MWS, RFS associated applications	
Transports	BCF EDDE	

Backbone
Network

Services	Description	Specifications
Domain Name Servers Routers - Wan Hub Routers Data Circuits	Network backbone systems will be available as required to provide access for the distributed systems and applications	Network backbone systems will be available 7X24

CUSTOMER SERVICE SUPPORT

Projected Workload. *

Helpline: 100 hours per month

45 - 50 calls per day (non-peak)

182 calls per day (peak) (month-end & year-end)

Non-helpline

Calls/contacts:

15 hours per month

1-2 calls per day

Task	Commitment
Service Hours	7:00 AM - 5:00 PM CST Monday through Friday
Reply	By 5:00 PM of the same business day
Progress Update	Within 60 minutes (first update) --or— Per time communicated during first update (subsequent updates)

*Note: In resolving IT Customer Service Helpline support calls, multiple meetings may occur, and initiation of a project request may result.

PRODUCTION SUPPORT

Projected Workload: 50 hours, 5-6 calls, per month

Task	Commitment
Service Hours (On-site)	7:00 AM – 5:00 PM CST
Service Hours (Off-site)	All other hours not on-site (through pager rotation)
Year-End Accounting Service Hours	24 hours per day
(On-site/Standby)	From the first through the fourth workday of the new year
Backlog (Severity Level 1)	0
Page/Return Phone Call (Primary)	Within 15 minutes
Progress Update	Within 30 minutes (first update) --or— Per time communicated during first update (subsequent updates)
Accounting Daily Batch Processing	By 8:00 PM CST
Completion	Monday through Friday
Accounting Notification	By 8:00 PM CST When Daily Batch Processing is not completed
Accounting Online Availability	24 hours Monday through Friday (Exceptions: reloads, 2:30 AM CST image copy)
Billing Daily Batch Processing	By 3:00 AM CST
Completion	Monday through Friday
Problem Review (Remedy)	By 10:00 AM CST Monday through Friday

Service Definitions

Communications

Service	Description	Specifications
Interactive Voice Response (IVR)	Customers are routed to the most effective method for receiving service. Customers receive updated messages regarding reported problems, servers, etc. Updated as events occur. Customers call X1234, the IT Response Center. Outside Metro area, call 1-800-ABC-HELP	Available 24 hours/day, 7 days/week, 365 days/year
Daily Processing Status Report	Daily report of operations events and status of jobs.	Available 6 AM sent via Voice Mail to selected Management/ Supervision.
Daily Output Status Report	Daily status report of hardware and applications.	Available 6 AM via IT operations home page, //WWW.INTRANET.COM/IT/ OPERATIONS/SUPPORT
Daily Problem Report	Daily report of management infrastructure problems.	Available 6 AM via IT Operations home page, //WWW.INTRANET.COM/ OPERATIONS/SUPPORT
Weekly Change Letter	This letter informs the client of weekend availability do to Change Management or Hardware Changes/ Improvements.	Available Friday 9 AM via IT Operations home page, // WWW.INTRANET.COM/ OPERATIONS/SUPPORT

Process Management

Service	Description	Specifications
Problem Management (see Problem Management Policy)	Problems escalated to IT Applications Development by calling X1234 must first be communicated through the Customer Service Center. IT provides application and technical support for all IT organizations within the stated times. Every effort will be made to isolate and repair problems.	Available Monday - Friday 7X24
Configuration Management	This agreement assumes that servers and workstations covered by this SLA will use approved change management practices.	Available Monday - Friday 8 AM - 4:30 PM Emergency changes available 24x7
Backup and Recovery	Standard tools will be used to support backup and recovery activities. Database and file backups of central system supported servers will be handled by IT based on application requirements.	Database recovery support will be provided for appropriately identified databases for the times stated. Recovery time depends on the size of files, databases and complexity of the recovery. Points of recovery are established by pre-existing backup and recovery processes.
Business Continuity	The best available solution will be used to provide availability based on Resources on hand at the time of Recovery. Recovery solutions will be assessed jointly by IT and the Business Unit Support areas to determine the best course of action.	Available Monday - Sunday 24 Hours
Change Management Policy (see Change Management Policy)	The Release Level Development (RLD) standards are expected to be followed for communication and scheduling changes to the application unless specific instructions are identified.	Available Monday - Friday 8 AM - 4:30 PM Emergency changes available 24x7

Service
Definitions

Service	Description	Specifications
Weekend Exceptions	Exceptions that will occur on the weekend are published in the weekend report	See Intranet Web page, //WWW.INTRANET.COM/ OPERATIONS/SUPPORT Available Friday 9 AM
Weekday Exceptions	When approved changes result in system unavailability during the normal availability window, a minimum of a two-workday advance notice will be provided	Available two days before changes are scheduled, Monday - Friday. See Intranet Web page, //WWW.INTRANET.COM/ OPERATIONS/SUPPORT

PROCESS IMPROVEMENTS

Projected Workload   200 hours per year*

*Process Improvements are classified as Project Requests. Further, Process Improvements are low in priority both within the Project Requests classification and within the working order across all classifications. Regardless, IT operations organization will devote a maximum of 200 hours per year on Process Improvements. All other Process Improvements will be prioritized and managed as defined in the Scope and Priorities section of this document.

Task	Commitment
Trend Analysis Findings and Recommendations Review	8:00 AM at the Status/ Review meeting on the second Tuesday of each month
Process Improvement and Implementation	200 hours per year

Metrics

Terminology

- Critical Level—Significant major impact to business units requiring immediate response.
- Problem Level—Possible impact to specific location/group requiring a quick response.
- Event Level—Minor to low problem to non-critical applications/systems, requiring a response.

Problem Escalation Matrix

Problem Status	Conditions	Resolution Team
Level IV	Any metric in unsatisfactory zone more then 2 days	IT Operations Manager Production Manager Logistics COF System Management
Level III	Any two metrics in the unsatisfactory zone. Any metric in the unsatisfactory zone more than one day	Production Manager Production Supervisor System Management
Level II	Any metric entering the unsatisfactory zone Any metric in the marginal zone more than two days	Production Supervisor Technical Analysts
Level I	Any metric entering the marginal zone	Technical Analysts

Reporting Procedures

- Metric Tracking Staff—Operations Resource Center
- Executive Review—Production Support Manager, Operations Manager
- Report Frequency—Daily, Weekly, Monthly
- Report Distribution—See report distribution list

Metric Standards	Performance Ranges		
	Acceptable	Marginal	Unsatisfactory
Technology Metrics			
Application Availability	97.5%	96%	94.5%
Applications Server Uptime	97.5%	96%	94.5%
Online System Average Response	Simple transaction < 1 sec Medium transaction < 2 sec Complex transaction < 5 sec		
System Backup	Daily	NO	Exceptions
Scheduled Output on Schedule			
Customer Support			
Help Desk Availability	99%	95%	90%
Average First Call Resolution Rate	70%	60%	50%
Average Call Management Closure Time	0 to 30 Minutes	30 Minutes to 1 Hour	1 Hour Plus
Customer Satisfaction			
Service Response Satisfaction			
Quarterly App Survey Satisfaction			

Priority of Service Requests

Priority Level	Description	Response Times	First Level Escalation Contact	Second Level Escalation Contact
Critical Level I	Significant to major impact to business. Affecting multiple systems/users. Problem affects a Business Vital System. May require action of multi-groups/departments for resolution	First 15 minutes	Help Desk Representative	Manager Help Desk
Critical Level II		15 - 60 Minutes	Manager Help Desk	IT Ops Executive
Critical Level III		1 - 4 Hours	IT Ops Executive	Business Systems Executive
Critical Level IV		4 Hours plus	Business Systems Executive	CIO

Priority of Service Requests (continued)

Problem Level I	Possible impact to specific location(s). May require action of multi-groups/ departments for resolution	30 Minutes	Help Desk Representative	Manager Help Desk
Problem Level II		30 - 60 Minutes	Manager Help Desk	IT Ops Executive
Problem Level III		1 - 4 Hours	IT Ops Executive	Business Systems Executive
Problem Level IV		4 Hours Plus	Business Systems Executive	CIO
Event Level I	May affect non-critical application/system(s). Minor to low visible problem.	1 Hour	Representative	Manager Help Desk
Event Level II		1 - 8 Hours	Manager Help Desk	IT Ops Executive
Event Level III		16 Plus Hours	IT Ops Executive	Business Systems Executive

Management Approval:_____Date:_____

Management Approval:_____Date:_____

Index

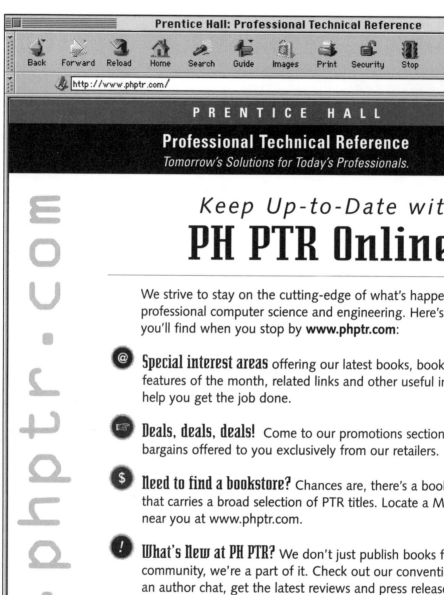